"In *Perpetual Revolt,* Jeff Nall asks us to "take deep breaths, long strides, and bold actions" to change the world in which we live. He challenges us to be "suspicious of passivity, of final responses, of ultimate goals and hints at utopias of any kind." And he warns us that all of this is likely to make us uncomfortable, even while we build a better world. Nall accomplishes these difficult tasks through strong, forceful writing and great insight and, most importantly, without embracing a cynical outlook. He blends a clarion call for social justice with a heartfelt desire to build a bridge between religious and secular progressives. *Perpetual Revolt* incites us to think big thoughts and will, I surmise, move many to take meaningful action."

> —*Michael Zimmerman, Dean of the College of Liberal Arts and Sciences,*
> *Butler University, and Founder, The Clergy Letter Project*
> *< www.evolutionsunday.org >*

"Jeff Nall's *Perpetual Revolt* is a well-written and insightful book. It is, in fact, really two books – one for the Peace and Justice movement based on his years of activism, and a second on the shared values of secular and religious progressives. In the first, Nall puts activism in its philosophical perspective, and does so with amazing wisdom, for one so young. But it is in the second part that Nall puts forth truths of great enduring value. With tenderness and clarity, he explains how the real battle in our society is not between believers and non-believers, but between the arrogant, pushy fundamentalists of either camp and those, whether atheist, devout Christian, or something else, who treat others with respect and dignity. The former make the most noise and get the most press, while the latter (though in the majority) get little notice. Nall calls for secular humanists and religionists to recognize their shared progressive values and engage in dramatic cooperation, relegating the fundamentalists of either kind irrelevant. This is a book that people of all faiths (or of none) can benefit from."

> —*Dr. Robert M. Bowman, Lt. Col., USAF, retired.*
> *(Dr. Bowman has been a full-time peace and justice activist for 26 years and is the*
> *Primate Archbishop of the United Catholic Church. A retired military officer and*
> *disabled combat veteran, Dr. Bowman spent 22 years in the Air Force where he flew*
> *101 combat missions in Vietnam. Presently, he is National Commander of "The*
> *Patriots" < www.thepatriots.us >, and President of the Institute for Space and Secu-*
> *rity Studies. He holds a PhD. in Aeronautics and Nuclear Engineering from Cal*
> *Tech. Dr. Bowman has received numerous awards such as the George F. Kennan*
> *Peace Prize, the President's Medal of Veterans for Peace, and the Air Medal with*
> *five oak leaf clusters. He has appeared on the McNeil-Lehrer News Hour, ABC*
> *News, the Larry King Show, Donohue, and Firing Line.)*

"*Perpetual Revolt* is a book that is greater than the sum of its parts. Jeff Nall's excellent essays against violence and war when read together have a profound impact, and his extensive knowledge of political and philosophical history becomes apparent. His writings on a proposed alliance of secular and religious progressives leaves the reader with hope and a sense of direction. Both secular and religious humanists will be better equipped for the struggle against violence and war once they have read *Perpetual Revolt.* They will have a clearer perception of the problems they face and of the advantages they may find in working together."

> —*James Rowe Adams, Founder and Honorary Advisor, The Center for Progressive*
> *Christianity < www.tcpc.org >; author, "From Literal to Literary: The Essential*
> *Reference Book for Biblical Metaphors," (2nd ed., Pilgrim Press)*
> *< www.BiblicalMetaphors.com >*

The ink in our pen
and the promises of our words
are only as meaningful
as our will to act is bold and undeterred.
– Jeff Nall

Perpetual REVOLT

REVOLT

*Essays on Peace & Justice and
the Shared Values of Secular,
Spiritual, & Religious Progressives*

JEFF NALL

ΩMEGA EDITIΩNS / PUBLIC REVΩLT
AN IMPRINT OF HOWLING DOG PRESS

FIRST EDITION
ISBN 10: 1-882863-92-5
ISBN 13: 978-1-882863-92-1

BOOK DESIGN & FINAL EDITS: MICHAEL ANNIS
COVER PHOTO: JOSEPH NALL; PHOTO MANIPULATION: JEFF NALL
COPY EDITING: ELIZABETH NALL
EDITING ASSISTANCE: APRIL L. NALL

ART CREDITS

Art for "Revealing the Revolutionary King" by Hope
Art for "Blood on Our Hands, U.S. Bombs and the Civilians They Kill"
by Greg Rebis
Art for "The U.S. Army, A Class Action Suit Waiting to Happen" by Hope
Art for "The Religious Right: Corrupting the Cross and the Constitution"
by Charley Deppner
All photos taken by Jeff Nall unless otherwise noted.

SPECIAL THANKS TO:

My wife, April, for the artistic advice, perceptive feedback, dedicated love and constant encouragement; my daughter, Charlotte, for motivating my conscience and my sense of purpose; and my anti-war family (Patriots for Peace) in Brevard County, Florida, for years of love, hope and support—especially Michele, Mike, Spence, and Vicki.

ΩMEGA EDITIΩNS / PUBLIC REVΩLT
AN IMPRINT OF HOWLING DOG PRESS
WWW.HOWLINGDOGPRESS.COM
WRITINGDANGEROUSLY@HOWLINGDOGPRESS.COM
Series DESIGNED & EDITED by MICHAEL ANNIS
PRINTED & PUBLISHED AT HOWLING DOG PRESS, U.S.A.

FOR MY GRANDMOTHER, CHARLOTTE E. NALL.

A person's accomplishments rarely belong to him alone.
Few achieve great heights without the love and support
of family and friends.

Perpetual

REVOLT

Words to Live By

"There is no final revolution; no final number" — Zamyatin

"Freedom only comes through persistent revolt, through persistent agitation, through persistently rising up against the system of evil." — Martin Luther King

"The world is kept alive only by heretics: the heretic Christ, the heretic Copernicus, the heretic Tolstoy. Our symbol of faith is heresy." — Zamyatin

"Nothing is sufficient for the man to whom the sufficient is too little" — Epicurus

"Ensure that you view both pleasure and pain as an inevitable tribute which wisdom itself must pay to human weakness." — Condorcet

WHAT LIES WITHIN

Over the last five years I have written extensively for independent media publications including the *Humanist*, *Toward Freedom*, *Z magazine*, *IMPACT Press* and *Clamor*. *Perpetual Revolt* is comprised of a variety of pieces derived from this publishing experience. The work is divided into two distinct yet intimately connected categories. The first section, "Fighting for Peace and Justice," includes a profile of the less talked about positions of Rev. Martin Luther King ("Revealing the Revolutionary King"), observations of anti-war protests in Washington, DC ("Ending the War Now: A Look at Recent Anti-War Protests"), and interviews with renowned independent journalist and writer, Amy Goodman, and legendary peace musician, Jesse Collin Young. Then there's "The U.S. Army, A Class Action Suit Waiting to Happen," a bold essay that poses the thought, if we can sue cigarette companies for false advertisement and targeting the youth with their lethal product, maybe we do the same to the United States Army military. In "Stopping the War Now: Peace Activists Meet with Pro-War Congressman" I highlight a Florida anti-war group's confrontation with a pro-war congressman.

The second half of the work focuses on the important task of putting an end to the divide among secular and religious progressives by realizing the humanism that unites the two groups. The work details the rarely discussed work of progressive Christians in developing the foundation for the separation of church and state ("The Religious Right: Corrupting the Cross and the Constitution"). It also features several interviews I conducted with Christian and atheist activists who discuss issues such as religion and science, creating alliances, dogmatism and free thought, religious fanaticism, and a surprising number of shared values. This section also features one of my better known essays, "Overcoming Antagonistic Atheism to Recast the Image of Humanism," which confronts those in the secular-humanist community who wish to fertilize discord rather than foster unity and mutual respect. There's even a creative rereading of Mel Gibson's *Passion of the Christ* that offers a different way of viewing the bloodletting film to reflect the torturous treatment of victims of United States aggression.

PHILOSOPHY OF PERPETUAL REVOLT

Perpetual Revolt denotes my philosophical, political, and written maturation. Many associate maturity with the process of becoming increasingly cynical and resigned to accept things the way they are. Reaching maturity for me, however, is the discovery and development of what I would call a philosophy of Perpetual Revolt. This philosophy is the product of my activist experience in the anti-war movement and my intellectual experience with the writings of a great many thinkers including the ancient Greek philosophers Heraclitus and Epicurus, French author and philosopher, Albert Camus, Rev. Dr. Martin Luther King Jr., Palestinian American activist and intellectual, Edward W. Said, and 20th-century Russian literary intellectual, Zamyatin.

Perpetual Revolt is a willingness to accept that heresy is required against the forces of today's status quo. In his 1919 essay, "Tomorrow," Zamyatin wrote that "eternal dissatisfaction is the only pledge of eternal movement forward, eternal creation." Moreover, he wrote that heretics like Christ, Copernicus, and Tolstoy keep the world alive. Today's heresy is an insistence that we forsake comfortable middles for daring sides and demand our nation respect the human rights of others around the world and respect universality in matters of international law, to name just two important issues. Just as former supporters of Soviet-Russian communism eventually repudiated its end-all-be-all mentality, we in the United States must recognize the failures of pure, free-market fundamentalist capitalism and realize, as Zamyatin wrote, "There is no final revolution, no final number." The world is always changing and we must find a new middle between the horrors of U.S.S.R. communism and U.S. capitalism. A struggle for equity and justice that ignores economic injustice is too apathetic to accomplish anything of substance. As Rev. Martin Luther King Jr. said, "Communism forgets that life is individual. Capitalism forgets that life is social. The kingdom of brotherhood is found neither in the thesis of Communism nor the antithesis of Capitalism but in a higher synthesis. It's found in a higher synthesis that can combine the truths of both."

Zamyatin was principally concerned with what he saw as the forces of entropy (the thermodynamic concept of energy moving toward rest). He was concerned with those wishing to reach the conclusion, to uncover artistic, social, even scientific finality. He actually witnessed this desire and tendency in Russia when the Stalinist regime put great effort into constraining the imagination of many of the very creative minds who had initially supported the Russian revolution. Zamyatin's ideas date back to at least ancient Greece when Heraclitus noted that fire was the most basic element of the universe. On a more abstract level of understanding, Heraclitus' view of fire as the universe's most fundamental building block referred to the fact that the flame of perennial change is the only constant the universe has to offer. In short, according to Diogenes Laertius' work, *Lives and Opinions of Eminent Philosophers*, Greek philosopher, Heraclitus held that "Nothing endures but change." So even when cultures resist change, the world around them, indeed the very universe in which they live continues on in a state of flux. For Zamyatin, the heretic is one who understands that both the beauty and the reality of existence requires the acceptance of constant change. In this way, Perpetual Revolt acknowledges that change is the only constant in the universe, and that only a life of struggle can compliment this reality. For serenity and perfect peace are elements of only death's domain.

In a similar vein, Said urged intellectuals to be on the front of the curve of change. (Italian philosopher Antonio Gramsci believed that all people are intellectuals in that we all possess rational faculties.) In the same way Zamyatin feared the forces of entropy, Said believed that intellectuals must oppose the forces of inertia which exalt the status-quo and thus misguide the charging train that is life.

What we know is that the moment an idea becomes canonized as dogma, be it rigid communism or rigid free-market capitalism, that idea poses a threat to the reality of constant change.

The trouble with renouncing dogma and accepting the reality of constant change in the universe, of course, is that we must accept the reality that nothing is everlasting. This idea is not only disturbing to many, it can literally be accused of collapsing the institution of hope. But it should not. The problem with our desire for eternal truths and eternal existences is that the universe refuses stasis. In order to "arrive," be it intellectually, politically or otherwise, human beings are forced to ignore *new* and sometimes temporary truths and the sanguinary consequences of their calcification: lives turned to corpses against the hard rock of their obstinate prejudices and principles. Instead, in order to keep alive the things most sacred to us, we must be ever vigilant and ever evolving – a fearless state of Perpetual Revolt.

Perpetual Revolt is suspicious of passivity, of final responses, of ultimate goals and hints at utopias of any kind. Instead, it recognizes diversity and divergence; it sees the good life, the democratic life as one which constantly evolves to face new challenges and erect new, better goals. Perpetual Revolt holds confrontation and non-violent conflict as virtues. Perpetual Revolt acknowledges human imperfection, lauds humility, and realizes that death is a kind of command to make use of our limited existence in this life. Indeed, death is not a call for fatalism as some will tell you; rather it is a siren screaming for action, for the pursuit of justice. Just as the person who knows well the desperation of poverty is more likely to appreciate a regal hotel or fine dinner than the wealthy man who is accustomed to a lavish lifestyle; those who accept that death casts his shadow upon us each and every day are most likely to know life's true and complete beauty. With this in mind, Perpetual Revolt demands that we accept that all life perishes and that death always looms. This weight, however, is less a burden than an inspiration: it gives us a sense of purpose, a sense of urgency. In this way we learn the beauty of the moment; but also acknowledge that well-lived moments, whether we

17

are present or not can lead to historical movements. By embracing the world before our very eyes and beneath our fingers and noses, we have a great chance to perish proudly "declaring in a beautiful song of triumph how well we have lived," as Epicurus put it. Moreover, by giving up our fear of death, according to Epicurus we free our minds and hearts to "live as a god among men; for man loses all semblance of mortality by living in the midst of immortal blessings."

Perpetual Revolt chides the complacency of those who give up a life of struggle—the only means to accomplish anything of value— for retired nonexistances, for giving up a life of meaning for a deadening consumerism and tepid comfort. If for no other reason than to justify restful sleep and a contented conscience; if for no other reason than to prove our loyalty to humanity, to that often ambiguous yet sacred ideal of justice; if for no other reason than to live as a god among mortals, Perpetual Revolt demands that we truly *live*, not merely exist, while occupying space on this planet. Finally, Perpetual Revolt realizes that what we do, not merely what we think or say, is what gives life true beauty and meaning. According to German political philosopher, Hannah Arendt, when we do not make our principles manifest via action then they do not exist. Addressing the subject of "freedom" in her work, *Between Past and Future*, Arendt argues that in the world of actuality, of material reality, what is comfortably sleeping in our hearts and minds means nothing if not expressed physically to the best of our abilities. The manifestation of our principles, however, brings our ideals, our principles into existence and gives even an idealist the opportunity to participate in creating new truths. She wrote: "Freedom or its opposite appears in the world whenever such principles are actualized; the appearance of freedom, like manifestations of principles, coincides with the performing act." In this way, we might go beyond Arendt's assertion to conclude that the principled but silent are complicit in that which they disagree with but do not assertively condemn. Similarly, French philosopher, John-Paul Sartre wrote: "There is no reality except in action." Believing that human beings possess the freedom to decide who they will become, he writes: "Man is nothing else than his plan;

he exists only to the extent that he fulfills himself; he is therefore nothing else than the ensemble of his acts, nothing else than his life." Alas, the ink in our pens is only as meaningful as our will to act out our ideals.

I believe that this view of life is essential to living and acting justly in 21st century United States. While I write this amid a historical and heated 2008 election that promises to "change" what must be viewed as nothing short of a period of perpetual war-mongering, dishonesty, and intellectual corruption, the promise of Democratic control of our government is but one step in the "left" direction. In reality, the Democrats are as responsible as the Republicans for the most serious problems in this country: our grotesque military spending; our fanatical and amoral if not immoral foreign policy; our willingness to allow corporations and the wealthiest of citizens dominate our "Democracy"; our treatment of women and minorities; our education system and so on. The struggle to create a better world does not hinge on elections. Presidential elections are merely a stepping stone, one which we should, indeed, use. The larger picture, however, requires that we understand that the struggle to implement such a vision is never totally won. The forces of hatred and fear and intolerance will never relent. Once we realize this, we then accept that the struggle for peace and justice and the ideal of humanity is not a campaign to win and then ignore, but instead an effort which defines our way of life. In short, I believe it is a way of life which requires Perpetual Revolt on the part of those who believe the only purposeful life is one which seeks to make the world better than it is. With every breath comes an opportunity, an obligation to remake the world into a more humane place. *Let us take deep breaths, long strides, and bold actions!*

Re: Christian Baep notion of ultimate
life purpose

DRESSED FOR DEATH, ARMED WITH WORDS

I always dress to greet death so that he will never catch me off guard.

So many turn from his beauty, shocked by his dress,
      but I savor and entreat that sweet bitterness.

Our lives are fleeting, this no one can escape, but death's incentive
      is one God nor heaven could create

Impermanence is that reminder that roses will die, and this life
      is but a short flicker in an eternal night

So I shackle my fears and arm my thoughts with words, it is better
      to suffer failure than live enslaved with regret

How many miserable moments alone have we endured; how many
      lives, serving silence, have been coldly squandered

There is a blasphemy greater than that of disbelief in God, the
      blasphemy of betraying our human vitality for contrived idols

Whether they are old haunting lovers who deprive us of new
      beginnings, or stoic educations that program us to distrust
      our desires

But death reminds me never to withdraw, when granted a chance
      at beauty and love I seek to be enthralled

To do otherwise would be to live dead, to find perfect beauty
      in a life not led.

And for those who think me irrationally driven by emotion,
      I offer no excuse, just a kind rebuke:

What good is living if we live suffocated by regret? If we spend
      so much time protecting ourselves with silence
      that our joys become mute?

There is something to be said for the heretic's hammer, that small dose
      of insanity which frees us from becoming living stone:

That which is alive but calcified, caged by the corpses of dead ideals
      and soon, their bones

Sometimes heresy is a willingness to believe that true living
      is taking chances, making leaps,
ending silence with fearless, risky speech

FIGHTING FOR PEACE & JUSTICE

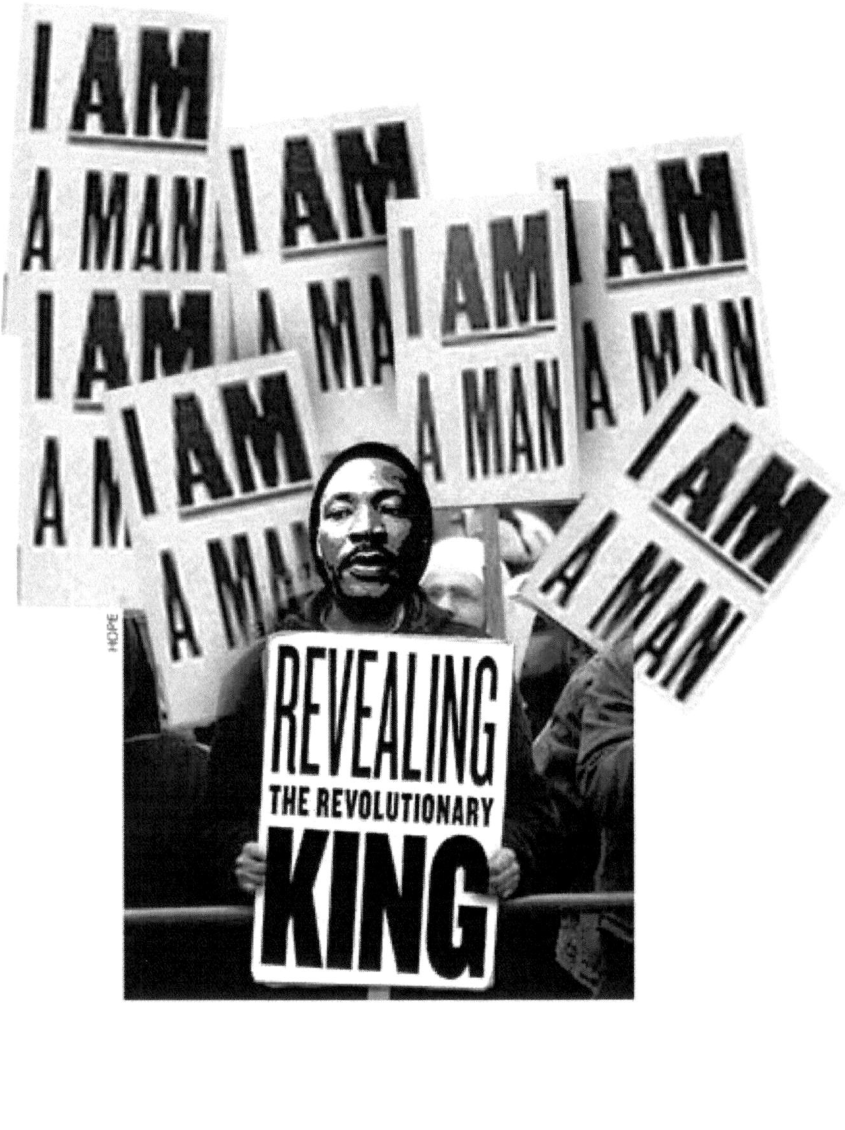
I AM
A MAN
REVEALING
THE REVOLUTIONARY
KING

REVEALING THE REVOLUTIONARY KING

⟩⟨

Dr. Martin Luther King has been dead for more than 35 years. Today, the blood of torture victims from Guantanamo to Bagram is seeping into his grave while another sarcastic procession of politicians praise the polite Negro civil rights advocate. They obscure his true epitaph, a radical vision of peace and justice, with profane flowers of hypocrisy and greed; drown his legacy in the putrid Katrina waters of class war and blatant racism; and molest his message of love with oil interests, foreign wars and gun-barrel liberation. In short, as another April denotes the death of the man, Martin Luther King, so too does it commemorate the assassination of his very spirit.

But the time has come to stop giving lip service to the whitewashed version of King that the powers that be force-feed us each year, and to take his call to march upon the radical road of living to free humanity of its bondage. We must resurrect the revolutionary King who called on America to give up its materialism, its objectification of human beings; the King who committed himself to economic and social equality for *everyone*; who unequivocally denounced warfare; repudiated neo-liberalism and an unrestrained, capricious capitalism. We must resurrect the spirit of the man who called on this nation to be "born again" because now more than ever, our country needs redemption, needs a savior, a prophet, needs the radical egalitarian message of Martin Luther King.

there is a danger in looking for the man on the white horse?

23

WAR IS NOT PEACE

After more than a decade of serious contemplation, King unwaveringly concluded that no war is worth sacrificing children to. He said, "More and more I have come to the conclusion that the potential destructiveness of modern weapons of war totally rules out the possibilities of war ever serving again as a negative good." These were not the words of a foolish idealist, but instead, those of an educated man, aided with as much if not more philosophical and historical wisdom, not to mention real-world experience, than anyone in the U.S. Senate or White House today. And while we often hear his name, most Americans–of all races–fail to adequately honor his legacy. To truly honor King, we must renounce war and prejudice, not simply read, watch, quote or reflect on his famous "I Have A Dream" speech. That's just the starting point.

The problem with the way great people like King are honored is that their images are polished and cleaned for the masses. These Rockwellian images of picturesque people are then sold to the public as something they had always loved. In truth, King sacrificed himself for the sins of a bigoted nation; rather than coddling the American people, he challenged the white, indolent masses to be better human beings, to reach beyond their own self-interest. He also challenged African American civil rights advocates to look beyond their personal struggle, and stand up against the Vietnam War.

Nothing exemplifies the distortion of King's legacy more fully than when President Bush made a mockery out of the 2003 MLK Day. Before the invasion of Iraq, Bush honored King's day while simultaneously preparing to wage a preemptive war. He even evoked King's own words, "Injustice anywhere is a threat to justice everywhere," implying that King would have supported the decision to go to war. Bush went on to say, "As Americans celebrate the 18th national commemoration of the life and legacy of this great leader, we recognize the lasting truth of his words and his legacy…" Nothing could be further from the truth. Ironically, the president, like many before and after him, used the words of a peacemaker as a slogan for impulsive, hegemonic military action.

Adding to his resume of hypocrisy and doubletalk, Bush recently managed to bastardize both King and Mahatma Gandhi's legacy of peacemaking, evoking their names while securing a nuclear deal with India. On March 2, 2006, Bush visited Gandhi's memorial where he bowed his head, laid a wreath and sprinkled petals at the site. The following day, while announcing a deal that would allow India access to nuclear fuel and technology, Bush praised Gandhi's legacy of peace and his influence on MLK: "India in the 21st century is a natural partner of the United States because we are brothers in the cause of human liberty. Yesterday, I visited a memorial to Mahatma Gandhi, and read the peaceful words of a fearless man. His words are familiar in my country because they helped move a generation of Americans to overcome the injustice of racial segregation. When Martin Luther King arrived in Delhi in 1959, he said to other countries, 'I may go as a tourist, but to India, I come as a pilgrim.'" Bush, on the other hand, goes to the memorials of peacemakers as a pilgrim, but nevertheless leaves a baffled tourist.

But Bush is not alone in this campaign of distorting peace as war. Earlier this year, planners of the San Antonio MLK day march, the largest such event, joined Bush in ignoring King's militant stance against war, when they voted overwhelmingly in favor of a military flyover by two fighter jets. The MLK Commission's decision incensed peace activists who complained that the flyover was a direct offense to King's complete rejection of warfare. Consternated by the opposition's complaints, Rev. Herman Price, the chairman of the city's MLK Commission, said, "They say the planes represent war and bombs and death, but at the same time those planes can also represent our freedom and peace." And Sheila McNeil, City Councilwoman for the district that the march traveled through, added: "[The Military] are the reason why we have peace, and this is MLK's peace march." Apparently the good reverend and Ms. McNeil have been listening too much to President Bush's beloved mantra, "peace is war, war is peace," and not enough to King's own words.

To revive King's spirit, we should begin by touting his emphatic opposition to the military-industrial-complex, which ordinary Americans support each tax year. With the U.S. spending more than the next 14 top military spenders in the world combined (two-fifth's of global spending), Americans would do well to recall these words from King:

> This business of burning human beings with napalm, of filling our nation's homes with orphans and widows, or injecting poisonous drugs of hate into the veins of peoples normally humane, of sending men home from dark and bloody battlefields physically handicapped and psychologically deranged, cannot be reconciled with wisdom, justice and love. A nation that continues year after year to spend more money on military defense than on programs of social uplift is approaching spiritual death.

As we continue to spend more than $400 billion dollars on our military (the president has asked for $462.7 billion for 2007) and less than $150 billion on education, health and human services, and the International Assistance Programs combined, that spiritual death looms terrifyingly near. Perhaps the best defense against terrorism would be to punish the warmongers who mar our democracy and threaten democratically elected leaders around the world whom they deem unacceptable, such as Venezuela's Hugo Chavez. Whatever the solution to global terrorism, as King put it, one thing is certain, you can't make peace out of a lust and zeal for war:

> The large power blocs talk passionately of pursuing peace while expanding defense budgets that already bulge, enlarging already awesome armies and devising ever more devastating weapons... Before it is too late, we must narrow the gaping chasm between our proclamations of peace and our lowly deeds which precipitate and perpetuate war.

ONE FOR ALL AND ALL FOR ONE

In addition to saving King's message of peace from the war hungry, we must protect his vehement vision of equality for all from people like the homophobes who tried to prop-up their agenda on King's grave. In 2002, The Associated Press (AP) reported that a coalition of several organizations used the legacy of Martin Luther King to encourage voters to repeal Miami-Dade County's gay rights ordinance. According to AP, the group made a reproachful pamphlet complete with the sponsoring effigy of King and the words: "Martin Luther King Jr. would be OUTRAGED! If he knew homosexual extremists were abusing the civil rights movement to get special rights based on their sexual behavior."

Those who knew him best know better. On August 1, 2002, Coretta Scott King said, "I appeal to everyone who believes in Martin Luther King Jr.'s dream to make room at the table of brotherhood and sisterhood for lesbian and gay people." Similarly, she also said at the 25th anniversary luncheon for Lambda Legal Defense and Education Fund on March 31, 1998, "I still hear people say that I should not be talking about the rights of lesbian and gay people and I should stick to the issue of racial justice... But I hasten to remind them that Martin Luther King Jr. said, 'Injustice anywhere is a threat to justice everywhere.'"

Adding yet another frustrating layer to the tepid, trivial treatment of deceased visionaries, Coretta's own commitment to gay and lesbian equality was largely glossed over by the mainstream media. Luckily, Deb Price, writing for *The Detroit News*, set the record straight in her February 6, 2006 column, "King's widow showed equality applies to gays." In the piece, Price not only proves Coretta's commitment to gay and lesbian rights, she also tells of how, before the assault on gay rights in Miami-Dade, Coretta battled bigots in Tampa in 1994 over the same issue:

> Foes of a Tampa, Fla., gay rights ordinance knew whose voice carried the most weight on civil rights. So, in 1994, when they mailed pamphlets to voters and left fliers on windshields at black churches, they dared to claim, 'Martin Luther King Jr. would be outraged if he knew that homosexual extremists were abusing the civil rights movement. Sodomy is not a civil right.'

Absolutely not true, King's widow immediately corrected. Coretta Scott King fired off a letter to the people of Tampa, urging them "to vote 'no' on any and all attempts to deny the promise of America to any citizen..." In later years, she declared all discrimination "equally wrong" and stressed "there is a connection between the racist, the anti-Semite, the sexist and the homophobe. They all share a sick need to dehumanize some minority to make themselves feel more adequate."

Having lost her husband to hate violence, Mrs. King reached out to the parents of Matthew Shepard the day after he was brutally murdered for being gay. In lifting up gay people, Coretta Scott King left our nation an enduring message worthy of being engraved on every heart: "Like Martin, I don't believe you can stand for freedom for one group of people and deny it to others." Most recently, journalist Max Blumenthal reported that, during the Conservative Christian rally Justice Sunday II, speakers evoked the memory of King and equated his civil rights struggle with the religious right's own movement. According to Blumenthal, "Born-again Watergate felon Chuck Colson declared that the Christian right was doing nothing but 'giving voice' to Martin Luther King Jr.'s philosophy."

The religious right's business of hate and intolerance is about as far removed from King's message of love and tolerance as hell is from heaven. King reproached the religious zealots of the world who saw religion as a weapon of hate, used to divide human beings rather than unite them:

> But I know that love is ultimately the only answer to mankind's problems ... I've seen too much hate ... I say to myself that hate is too great a burden to bear. I have decided to love. If you are seeking the highest good, I think you can find it through love. The beautiful thing is that we aren't moving wrong when we do it because John was right, God is love. He who hates does not know God. He who loves has the key that unlocks the door to the meaning of ultimate reality.

THE FAILURES OF CAPITALISM

Beyond the issue of peace and brotherhood, perhaps the most neglected of King's views is his support for altering the U.S. economic system. At a time when a quarter of the world's financial assets belong to 8.3 millionaires and the U.S. Senate refuses to increase the $5.15-an-hour minimum wage, King's critique of capitalism has never been more relevant. He explained:

We must honestly admit that capitalism has often left a gulf between superfluous wealth and abject poverty, has created conditions permitting necessities to be taken from the many to give luxuries to the few, and has encouraged small hearted men to become cold and conscienceless so that, like Dives before Lazarus, they are unmoved by suffering, poverty-stricken humanity. The profit motive, when it is the sole basis of an economic system, encourages a cutthroat competition and selfish ambition that inspire men to be more I-centered than thou-centered.

Considering the increasing concentration of wealth among the few, it's no wonder King believed that American society needed to be restructured and called for a broader distribution of wealth. According to a study by the Annie E. Casey, Ford and Rockefeller foundations, "one in every five U.S. jobs pays less than a poverty-level wage for a family of four." As a result, the study concludes "that nearly 39 million Americans, including 20 million children, are members of 'low-income working families'—with barely enough money to cover basic needs like housing, groceries and child care." In his own day, King said that "an edifice which produces beggars needs restructuring" and seriously questioned claims of private ownership of natural resources.

See my friends, when you deal with this you begin to ask the question, who owns the oil? You begin to ask the question, who owns the iron-ore? You begin to ask the question why is it that people have to pay water bills in a world that's two-thirds water? ... Now don't think you have me in a bind today, I'm not talking about Communism ... My inspiration didn't come from Karl Marx. My inspiration didn't come from Engels; my inspiration didn't come from Trotsky; my inspiration didn't come from Lenin ... Communism forgets that life is individual. Capitalism forgets that life is social. The kingdom of brotherhood is found neither in the thesis of Communism nor the antithesis of Capitalism but in a higher synthesis. It's found in a higher synthesis that can combine the truths of both.

King went on to add that "the problem of racism, the problem of economic exploitation and the problem of war are all tied together. These are the triple evils that are interrelated."

THE COURAGEOUS CONSCIENCE

Above all else, King called on us to have a courageous conscience, unafraid of dissent or its consequence. When he was asked about his anti-war stand during the Vietnam War he answered simply: "Vanity asks the question 'Is it popular?' Conscience asks the question 'Is it right?'" It is time we make a serious commitment to taking over where Dr. King left off, by standing for free speech, economic equality, and human rights, despite the corporate media's influence on the American masses.

As we reflect on another lost year for King, a year he should've had a chance to experience, we are reminded that now a new shooter has taken aim at his very essence. King's legacy, the project of peace he left behind, is targeted for assassination and, with it, hope for a new nation. It's time to heed his call to service, to action. No longer should we mourn his death, but put our all into preserving his dream and applying his vision. On April 7, 1957, King gave an emotive, soul-driving description of the process of achieving freedom. In his speech, "The Birth of a New Nation," King declared:

> If there had not been a Gandhi in India with all of his noble followers, India would have never been free. If there had not been an Nkrumah and his followers in Ghana, Ghana would still be a British colony. If there had not been abolitionists in America, both Negro and white, we might still stand today in the dungeons of slavery. And then because there have been, in every period, there are always those people in every period of human history who don't mind getting their necks cut off, who don't mind being persecuted and discriminated and kicked about, because they know that freedom is never given out, but it comes through the persistent and the continual agitation and revolt on the part of those who are caught in the system. Ghana teaches us that.

So did Martin and Coretta. Now it's time to stick *our* necks out.

—Originally published in the Spring 2006 issue of IMPACT Press.

SACRIFICING LIBERTY FOR SECURITY:
THE NEW AMERICAN WAY?

>K

I recently learned that I have my own FBI file. You might be surprised to find out that your activities are being monitored, as well,
whether you feel they deserve to be or not. And, with Congress re-
storing nearly all of the PATRIOT Act's sun-setting provisions to their
scorching, oppressive noon day glory, the time has come to ask ourselves—has freedom finally fallen to the fatalistic tandem of fear and
security?

People like U.S. District Attorney of Massachusetts Michael J.
Sullivan don't think so. Earlier this year, Sullivan argued that the
"reauthorization of the USA PATRIOT Act will maintain the proper
balance between guarding our civil liberties and protecting our
homeland from those who seek to harm us" ("PATRIOT Act has not
hurt civil liberties," *The Standard-Times*, May 25, 2005). And Attorney
General Alberto Gonzales echoed the Bush administration, proclaiming that the PATRIOT Act is necessary to "protect our country
against another terrorist attack." ("Gonzales defends USA PATRIOT
Act," *The Advocate*, August 8, 2005). Others dismiss the ACLU's
claim that the FBI has made a habit of targeting groups and individuals because of their liberal brand of politics ("Documents Obtained
by ACLU Expose FBI and Police Targeting of Political Groups," ACLU

31

press release, May 18, 2005). Meanwhile, Bush supporters frequently complain that liberals are simply blowing things out of proportion and that the occasional intrusive measure is necessary in order to win the war on terrorism. I, however, fear the worst; that the brilliant blues of American pride are fading into the dull bruises of a nation that has lost its constitutional soul.

As an activist, I experienced, first-hand, the gross abuses such optimistic and faithful voices are deaf to. On January 20, 2005 I joined about three dozen peaceful demonstrators in taking to the streets of Melbourne, Florida, to mourn the reelection of President Bush. In a funeral-style procession, we walked down one of the city's central thoroughfares brandishing anti-Bush posters, a nine-foot banner that read, "not a mandate," and hand-crafted styrofoam headstones, commemorating the liberties eroding under the Bush administration.

The plan was to march from a nearby park to the local city hall. There we would break the headstones and refuse to bury our rights. But by the time we had arrived at city hall, about 45 minutes into the event, it was clear our rights had already been buried. Our group of about 36 protestors, including four children, a woman in a wheelchair, and at least four people over the age of 60, was met by nine city police officers. Worst of all, one police officer, a member of the crime scene investigation unit, was stationed across the street where he filmed the entire protest.

After the event, the Brevard County chapter of the ACLU obtained records about the police presence at the event. It turned out that former Melbourne police chief Keith Chandler had enacted a policy that made videotaping of anti-administration demonstrations a routine procedure. Chandler did so following the issuance of an FBI memo, in October 2003, which instructed law enforcement in the ways of monitoring legal protests. With the aid of an apologetic city of Melbourne police chief Don Carey, whose organization unintentionally recorded a suspicious SUV that turned out to be from the Brevard County Sheriff's Office (BCSO) and who implemented new rules to protect the exercise of free speech and discarded the routine videotaping policy, the ACLU discovered that the BCSO had co-ordinated intense, covert surveillance of the event.

The initial information released showed that officers, under the direction of Bruce Parker, Director of the Investigative Support Unit for the BCSO, photographed the license plates of demonstrators' parked cars, while others took photos of participants from the aforementioned unmarked SUV. At least one undercover officer infiltrated the demonstration. The sheriff's office even notified security at nearby Patrick Air Force Base about the event.

The BCSO had generated a list of six "persons of interest," a label often used when referring to suspected criminals. The records also showed that the BCSO had obtained the date of birth, social security number and address of each of the six listed persons. In my case, the BCSO directly referred to me as a "suspect," took down my car's VIN number, and had my email address.

In a follow-up records request, the BCSO released more than 500 pages revealing expansive surveillance operations around the entire county. The BCSO had not only spied on our demonstration, but had also conducted similar investigations of more than ten other protests. Beginning back in 2002, the officers took photos and did background checks on members of the Cape Canaveral Coalition for Racial Justice. They also monitored events organized by the Global Network Against Weapons and Nuclear Power in Space, the International Association of Longshoremen, and Patriots for Peace (PFP), which organized several pre-war peace demonstrations. In the case of PFP, a group I helped organize, the BCSO assigned an undercover officer to attend and report on peace rally planning meetings. To top it all off, the records revealed that my activism had somehow earned me an FBI number. (Even an issue of *IMPACT press*, which I had previously written for, was scanned and placed into the file.)

Not surprisingly, all of the groups the BCSO scrutinized were left-leaning organizations. In contrast, records show that BCSO attended only one right-leaning rally, "Rally for America," a support the troops/pro-Iraq war event. Though the event, held in March 2003, was attended by more than 1,000 people, BCSO took no photos and made no lists as it had done at other events. In fact, BCSO was actually present at the behest of the event's organizers who were concerned about potential counter-protestors.

When Bruce Parker attempted to publicly rebuff the accusation that the BCSO targeted liberal organizations, he only succeeded in solidifying his bias: "A pro-America rally does not attract anarchists to participate in the rally, except for those who might come to counter-protest. If they don't show up there, there's nothing to record [license] tags for. We're looking for anarchists that are going to commit violent acts" ("ACLU seeks reforms in county spy policy," *Florida Today*, May 16, 2005). Parker's comments beg the question, if anarchists wouldn't participate in a "pro-America" rally, why is he so convinced they'd participate in racial equality protests, peace demonstrations, and civil rights rallies? After all, what's more American than making use of the First Amendment and peaceably assembling? The answer lies with Sgt. Andrew Walters, the sheriff's spokesman. When asked what the six counter-inauguration participants, labeled "persons of interest," were of interest for, Walters said "Protesting in an anti-government assembly" ("Spying on citizens", *Florida Today*, March 23, 2005). Evidently, in the eyes of the sheriff's office, the only kinds of "pro-government" assemblies are cheerleading rallies praising the policies of the Bush administration.

In response to a torrent of media attention and fiercely critical newspaper editorials, Bruce Parker defended the surveillance tactics: "Before this last protest, demonstrators didn't even know we were present. We were there to make sure there were no protestors who could potentially be a problem, like a group of anarchists–to know who was there we had to get license tag numbers" ("Records reveal more spying," *Hometown News*, May 13, 2005). Parker said September 11 made such tactics necessary and even alluded to the fact his organization was working with the FBI: "We don't want there to be another September 11 where police agencies didn't do as much as they could do to follow up on leads that were available... If we find anything, we immediately take it to the FBI" ("ACLU seeks reforms in county spy policy," *Florida Today*, May 16, 2005).

Considering the instructions of the once classified 2003 FBI memo, it's pretty clear that the FBI is leading local law enforcement agencies, like the BCSO, down a blurry path where constitutional dissent begins to look like terrorism: "Law enforcement agencies should be alert to possible indicators of protest activity and report any potentially illegal acts to the nearest FBI Joint Terrorism Task Force." The Memo also advises: "Extremist elements may engage in more aggressive tactics that can include... trespassing, the formation of human chains or shields, makeshift barricades... peaceful techniques can create a climate of disorder."

In other words, agencies like the BCSO, likely acting on the FBI's directive to preemptively monitor the activities of lawful activists, are treating dissenters as they would terrorists. Epitomizing this purposeful convolution of the war on terror and a crackdown on dissent, Sheriff Jack Parker said this, in defending his organization's monitoring of the counter-inauguration rally: "We must both uphold the freedoms provided by the Constitution and at the same time protect the lives of our citizens. This is a delicate balance... Terrorists use anti-government activities to form alliances and recruit persons to perform acts of terrorism. If we did not take a special interest in activities that could attract terrorists, we would not be doing our job."

By equating First Amendment protected demonstrations to "anti-government activities" that attract terrorists, law enforcement leaders like Sheriff Parker prove to be inept defenders of the First Amendment. Blinded by ever-increasing policing powers, men like Bruce Parker can hardly tell the difference between ordinary Americans marching to preserve freedom and democracy in the U.S., and those associated with the Oklahoma City bombing. Responding to criticism over the surveillance of counter-inauguration protesters, Bruce Parker retorted, "We were trying to protect the citizens of the county. We want to make sure there is not another Terry Nichols among the protesters" ("Police had interest in war protestors," *Hometown News*, March 25, 2005).

By June 2005, Sheriff Parker had seemingly changed his tune, announcing that his agency would henceforth only gather intelligence on demonstrators who pose "an identifiable potential for violence." But the ambiguity of this language–what constitutes such "an identifiable potential"?–has satisfied few concerns, and raised new questions. Besides, with the PATRIOT Act fully renewed and back at his side, Guantanamo's the limit.

Though the ominous surveillance of lawful citizens in Brevard County has not yet been linked to the Patriot Act directly, Kevin Aplin, Vice-President of the Brevard ACLU, says one thing is certain: "We do know that the [Bush] administration has set a political climate where law enforcement feels emboldened to collect surveillance on First Amendment protected activities, using the war on terrorism as justification. The Sheriff here has said they're looking for terrorists. So they're certainly using the war on terror to justify collecting intelligence on citizens that have broken no laws and are engaging in lawful First Amendment activities."

While many in the community decried such egregious policing, many fully agreed that secret monitoring and otherwise unconventional tactics were necessary in the interest of safety. During a city council meeting on the subject, Melbourne Mayor Harry Goode commented that extreme security measures were sometimes necessary because terrorists want to destroy everything that is America. "This is a whole different United States than the one we grew up in," he said ("Police to stop videotaping protesters," *Florida Today*, February 23, 2005). Many Brevard County residents writing into the local paper agreed. Bill Logan wrote: "Knowing we are under tight security since 9/11, and also knowing there are terrorist cells within our borders, they don't stop to think why police were filming. It's for their own protection." Anthony Marchione wrote, "There are many legitimate reasons to use various surveillance methods, some of which are not necessarily open to public scrutiny" (Letters to the Editor, *Florida Today*, March 13, 2005).

With fear guiding so many toward faith in security, the U.S. may travel a path not unlike that prophesied by an 80-year-old dystopian novel, *We*. Written by Russian author Yevgeny Zamyatin, *We* tells the story of a society, the One State, that decides the "only means of ridding man of crime is ridding him of freedom." To achieve its utopian society of perfect peace, the One State eradicates individuality, privacy, and freedom; and the citizens exalt the Guardians (secret police), who monitor their every action, for "lovingly protecting" them.

As America flees the open skies of liberty for the patriarchal shelter of authoritarianism, perhaps it's only a matter of time before we turn to the transparent walls of the One State: "At all other times we live behind our transparent walls that seem woven of gleaming air—we are always visible, always washed in light. We have nothing to conceal from one another. Besides, this makes much easier the difficult and noble task of the Guardians. For who knows what might happen otherwise?"

—Originally published in the Fall 2005 issue of IMPACT press.

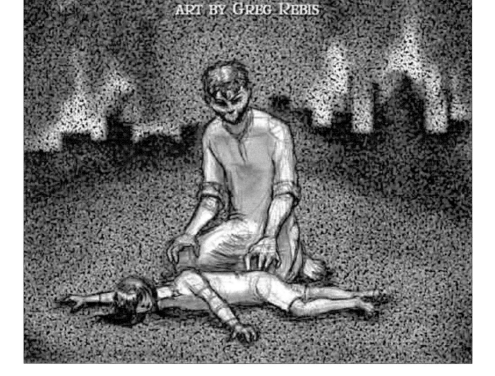

BLOOD ON OUR HANDS: U.S. BOMBS AND THE CIVILIANS THEY KILL

✝

A surreal sky bends you over your young child, a morbid tapestry: forlorn skin painted over in ash, her deadened innocence wafts putridly; charred wounds leave gaping holes in her bloodless body. Her vacant eyes are tragically buried in a cruel grave made of rubble and shrapnel, betrayed by the inhumanity, the indifference to life, of those that murdered her with such pinpoint accuracy. Among a mangled landscape of destruction, her tiny frame now lies, perverted by politics, ravaged by reasons, murdered by liberation, and wholly raped of life.

Those that have experienced the birth of their own child know that the profundity of such elevates an otherwise egotistical existence to a selfless one. Thus it takes little to no imagination to understand the sometimes vengeful nature of a parent experiencing the loss of a child and, in this case, one tragically caught between the bombs and mayhem of politics and warring parties. Whether an act of terrorism, or a virtuous attempt to liberate a people from the rule of a tyrant, once another man has taken your child's life, humanity becomes a luxury your heart cannot afford.

The 2002 movie *Collateral Damage*, starring Arnold Schwarzenzegger, is a good expression of this psychological turmoil. In the movie, Schwarzenzegger's character sets out to avenge the death of his wife and daughter, who were casualties of a terrorist's bomb-ing. This brand of American justice seems to appeal to many Ameri-cans, as the popularity of the movie would indicate; it has grossed more than $40 million in the U.S. alone. However, there is a flagrant sense of irony when one considers how Americans might respond to a Middle Eastern vigilante, like Arnold, who tries to get back at a U.S. military adviser who commanded some inexact "strategic" bomb-ing, which resulted in the death of *his* wife and child.

While the U.S., from Hollywood to Washington D.C., has always been quick to sympathize and console American indignation, border-ing on vigilantism, Americans have proven less apt to recognize simi-larities between their emotionalism and that of other nations and people with which they are involved. Whereas the tragic loss of life on September 11, 2001 precipitated a blank check for President Bush to hunt down terrorists, and even wage war in Iraq, Americans are not, in turn, willing to grant Iraqis, for example, the same right to indignation and fury. To date, many more civilians have died as a di-rect result of U.S. military intervention in Iraq than the number of innocent people that died in the Twin Towers. But not only has the press hardly spoken up on the issue of civilian deaths in Iraq, the U.S. is insisting that the number of those killed is not at all worth tally-ing–an attitude that will likely cultivate the same vigilantism por-trayed in the Schwarzenzegger movie.

Specifically, the December 10, 2003 article "No More Iraqi Casu-alty Counts?" by the Associated Press reported, "Iraq's Health Minis-try has ordered a halt to a count of civilians killed during the war and told its statistics department not to release figures compiled so far." Many war observers, like John Sloboda, co-founder and press spokesperson for IraqBodyCount.net [www.iraqbodycount.net/], are not the least bit surprised by the development. Sloboda says that he has no doubt the demand to stop the counting came directly from U.S. authorities in an effort to suppress further discontent among the indigenous population. "The general Iraqi population will be as keen to establish this figure as the U.S. population wished to know the death toll in 9-11," he explained. "It is inconceivable that an Iraqi would order the stopping of this count unless there was, metaphorically, a U.S. gun at his head."

The U.S. is a long-time opponent of counting civilian casualties resulting from its wars, instead promising to employ meticulous and lengthy measures to minimize such casualties. Sloboda says the country's policy of not tallying such figures is almost entirely politically motivated. Both the U.K. and the U.S. claim they do this because it is not possible to be totally accurate, and because "every reasonable effort was taken to avoid civilian casualties," Sloboda said. "The actual reasons relate to the management of domestic opinion. The U.S. will suppress any electorally inconvenient information. They also know that almost no head of state will dare to challenge them on this, neither will the U.N., nor the Red Cross. Even the U.S.'s critics, such as Putin, will never challenge the U.S. on civilian casualties, because there is similar blood on their own hands."

Historians have shown there are plenty of reasons for U.S. policy makers to avoid such morbid musings. The U.S. has, in part, been responsible for two million North Korean civilian deaths during the Korean War, and more than one million civilian deaths during the Vietnam War (*American Foreign Relations*, Clifford, et al., 2000). Other macabre statistics reflecting hundreds of thousands of civilian deaths resulting from U.S. military action, specifically the questionable use of the A-bomb on Hiroshima and Nagasaki in order to bring about "the end" of World War II, paint a horrific portrait of the consequences resulting from such action.

While the U.S. continues to refrain from such research, organizations like IraqBodyCount.net fill a void by maintaining a studious, in-depth account of the complete death toll in Iraq. To date, reports have consistently agreed that more than 3,000 Iraqi civilians have been killed. According to a detailed investigation by the Associated Press, at least 3,240 civilians have been killed, and those deaths only occurred between March 20 and April 20 of 2003. In fact, the investigation concluded that the total number of civilian deaths over the course of the war "was sure to be much higher" ("No More Iraqi Casualty Counts?" *Associated Press*, Dec. 10, 2003).

Still, IraqBodyCount.net indicates that U.S. bombing and other military action have likely led to more than 7,000 civilian deaths. Meanwhile, on Oct. 28, 2003, The Project on Defense Alternatives [http://www.comw.org/pda/], a Cambridge, Massachusetts think tank, reported an estimated "4,300 non-combatants were killed during the major combat phase of the war in Iraq" ("Iraq war killed 13,000, study finds," Agence France-Presse, Oct. 28, 2003). The group has also estimated that 3,500 Iraqi civilians were killed during the 1991 Gulf War.

The fact that such a greater number of Iraqi civilians have died as a result of an American invasion, again far greater than the number of American civilians that died during the September 11 tragedy, offers a disquieting juxtaposition. In considering the wrathful sentiments of Americans following the collapse of the Twin Towers—some believe such ire enabled the President to draw loose connections between Saddam and al-Qaida in order to get backing for the war against Iraq—one might warily consider whether those Iraqis who have lost loved ones have an equal right to resent the U.S. bombs, which perpetrated the majority of the civilian killings, as Americans resented the terrorists. Some question if, for instance, the U.S., fueled by righteous indignation, was correct in responding to thousands of American civilian deaths by waging war on those responsible.

Would the same principle of rightness in forceful action apply to Iraqis avenging the deaths of their loved ones? While most would argue that the U.S. had good intentions in overthrowing Saddam's regime, many fail to recognize that the parallel between the situations is that, in both cases, innocent people were obliterated. Such a realization drove a practically minded Martin Luther King to expound, "More and more I have come to the conclusion that the potential destructiveness of modern weapons of war totally rules out the possibilities of war ever serving again as a negative good."

Whereas politicians and analysts often measure the success of events like war in their totality, the roots of terrorism, incessant feuds among groups like the Palestinians and Jews, and even anti-Americanism often spring from sorrowful experiences among the populace during such altercations, which then fester and manifest in prolonged resentment. Though Americans might view the war as an overwhelming success, especially with the capture of Saddam, instances where the U.S. has attempted to kill Saddam and his sons by bombing public buildings or raiding homes are likely to exist equally in the conscious of the people.

Attempts to kill leaders and figures of great importance–decapitation attacks, as they are called–have been determined to be responsible for a significant number of the total civilian casualties. According to a story reported on Dec. 12, 2003 by *OneWorld.net*, an online news agency, the New York-based organization, Human Rights Watch had recently determined that "Hundreds of civilians were killed by Coalition cluster bombs and air strikes designed to decapitate the Iraqi leadership." The article went on to explain that while the report had "found that U.S.-led Coalition forces in Iraq generally tried to comply with international humanitarian law, nonetheless concluded that U.S. ground forces were too eager to use cluster munitions in populated areas, and that 50 decapitation attacks failed to hit a single one of their targets, but caused dozens of civilian deaths and injuries" ("Cluster Bombs, Decapitation Bombing Killed Hundreds of Iraqis, Says Human Rights Watch," OneWorld, Dec. 12, 2003)

In one specific incident in the Baghdad district of Mansur, reporter Robert Fisk writes that "dozens of Iraqi civilians including women and children were killed as a result of such attempts to kill the former dictator and company" ("US troops turn botched Saddam raid into a massacre", The Independent, July 28, 2003). Even more recently, in Afghanistan a "U.S. airstrike aimed at a wanted Taliban commander mistakenly killed nine children in an Afghan mountain village" ("U.S. Strike Kills 9 Afghan Kids," Associated Press, Dec. 7, 2003). Although the U.S. government might believe such actions are necessarily conjoined in their effort toward rooting out tyrannical, terrorist forces, the families forced to endure the loss of sons and daughters might envisage the source of tyranny as a red, white, and blue flag.

Interestingly, while many might first point to the callousness of the State Department and the Bush administration in their willingness to sacrifice civilian lives to accomplish mission objectives, Sloboda is fast to relieve Bush and his Republicans as they are only bearers of guilt and responsibility for the death toll. Instead, he holds the American people, in part, accountable, and also Democrats, for refusing to take earnest interest in the mounting civilian death toll in Iraq. "It was exactly the same in Vietnam," he complained. "This is nothing to do with George Bush or the Republicans. It is endemic to U.S. society at all levels. Even a so-called anti-war Democratic candidate, such as Howard Dean, ignores Iraqi civilian casualties. In November, he distinguished himself by saying, "There are 400 people dead who would not be if we hadn't gone to war." Of course, the real number of dead is over 20,000. The 400 refers to Americans. Of all the Democratic candidates, only one mentions Iraqi civilian casualties as a reason for criticizing the invasion, Dennis

Kucinich. All the rest care as little about casualties as the Republicans."

While the White House has its eye on the prize of rooting out Iraqi insurgency, quelling unrest, and nation-building, the worldwide patrons to this Iraqi-theater are not likely to dismiss the importance of counting the dead bodies of innocent men, women, and children. Alas, though powerful figures in and outside of both Iraq and the U.S. have decided to "halt" the measure of civilian death, the American public *is* likely to measure the success and progress of the Iraqi campaign in body bags. While Sloboda agrees, he is quick to point out cynically, "but only American body bags."

Though the U.S. is likely to escape the scrutiny of most of its citizens and many of the world's leaders, there are those who believe that persons responsible for so many civilian deaths, possibly as many as 10,000, perpetrated in a pre-emptive war, are nonetheless war criminals. Interestingly, before the end of September, National Public Radio (NPR) featured a special on Errol Morris's forthcoming documentary, *The Fog of War*, which features a candid series of interviews with former Secretary of Defense Robert S. McNamara. In the film, McNamara calls the viewer's attention to the barbaric repose with which one kills, once caught in the game of war. According to NPR, in the film, McNamara, a military officer and aid to General Curtis LeMay, whose forces conducted the fire-bombings and atomic bombings of Japanese cities during World War II, shares a hard learned lesson on the horrors of war: "The human race prior to that time and today has not really grappled with what are, I'll call it, the rules of war," said McNamara. "Was there a rule then that says you shouldn't bomb, kill, burn-to-death 100,000 civilians in a day?"

While the U.S. did not drop an A-bomb on Iraqi civilians in the second Gulf War, similar questions are being raised today. Specifically, Sloboda points to recent reports by Human Rights Watch, detailing deaths that resulted from practices that he says border on war crimes. "One clear category of potential war crimes relates to the use of cluster bombs," he said, "which, by their nature, kill civilians indiscriminately." In fact, according to a press release by Human Rights Watch, which discusses the finding of their 147-page report,

> Hundreds of civilian deaths in the U.S.-led invasion of Iraq could have been prevented by abandoning two misguided military tactics. The use of cluster munitions in populated areas caused more civilian casualties than any other factor in the coalition's conduct of major military operations in March and April. U.S. and British forces used almost 13,000 cluster munitions, containing nearly 2 million submunitions, that killed or wounded more than 1,000 civilians. ("The Conduct of the War and Civilian Casualties in Iraq," Human Rights Watch, Dec. 12, 2003).

That U.S. and British policies–the disinterest in tallying civilian deaths and the use of munitions in "populated areas"–so greatly discount the value of individual lives, one must wonder if McNamara's words are as applicable to the situation in Iraq as they are to World War II and Vietnam. While the U.S. will most certainly be exempt from any criminal charges–regardless of the profusion or validity of such accusations–associated with the most recent Gulf War, McNamara's analysis of the World War II bombing strategies may also be an implicit indictment against the U.S.'s cluster bombing tactics. "Lemay said, 'If we'd lost the war we all would have been prosecuted as war criminals'. And I think he's right."

—Originally published in the February-March 2004 issue of IMPACT press.

JOIN!

JOIN!

JOIN!

The
U.S. Army

A Class Action Suit
Waiting to Happen

by JEFF NALL

HOPE

THE U.S. ARMY: A CLASS ACTION SUIT WAITING TO HAPPEN

⽊

An indignant, emotionally discountenanced parent of a former smoker walks out of a courtroom in Los Angeles to greet an audience of media personnel. He wears a proud smile, with wavering lips, and is caught between tears of joy and tears of anger.

On this day, a jury has passed judgment in his favor against big tobacco, proclaiming the company that produced the cigarettes used deceptive advertisement and irresponsibly withheld important information concerning factors of risk involved in participating in the act of smoking.

Jack's son Tom died as a result of a cancer that spread through his body until life escaped each of his pores. The allure of smoking—its social trappings, its flavor, its affect, its commercial appeal, its image as portrayed by decades of advertisement—lent Tom the motives to begin a hazardous career of smoking, which he ended in the glorious clutches of an IV and a hospital bed.

While the above story is but a fictitious illustration of the modern plight consumers and purveyors of tobacco face, the fact is, according to the *Los Angeles Times*, in Oregon alone "two cases filed by families of deceased smokers produced damage awards totaling $180 million" ("Ex-Smoker Wins Tobacco Suit", September 27, 2002).

Now, I ask that those with a propensity to abstract thought replace the plaintiff with a family whose son or daughter has died in combat fighting a war in Iraq or protecting other foreign interests abroad. Furthermore, replace the defendant with the United States Army.

Seems like a stretch, you decide, responding aloud, "Soldiers willingly participate in joining the military. They also enjoy benefits, training and are paid very well." But, I ask, is it really hard to fathom? One of the main reasons tobacco companies are forced to pay inordinate amounts of money to plaintiffs is because many courts have decided their former methods of advertisement and lack of warnings were adverse. Tobacco companies purposely omitted truths about the affects smoking could have on individuals; moreover they attempted to lure young impressionable people to a "pleasurable" activity via a potent ad campaign. Tobacco advertisements listed all the good and left the bad up to self-evident cognition. "The military doesn't do that," many may remark. But upon closer examination, there appears to be some similarity between the two.

One of the best examples of such activity is found in the ranks of the Army. The new ad campaign—most have almost surely heard of—is themed "an Army of One." Literature on this "Army of One" can be found at many high schools and on college campuses. In reading through the literature there is no mention of the perils that await those who enlist. Page after page speaks of the incentive to pay off college loans, receive medical and dental care and earn thousands of dollars each year. To many Americans this may sound like a dream come true. But if people are lured into a hazardous career in the military that may very well end in death, all because of a keen, misleading ad campaign, is the U.S. military—like big tobacco—liable for those deaths?

At one point, towards the end of one brochure found at a Central Florida community college, potential recruits are reminded of the opportunity to earn incentives totaling up to $85,000. Another pamphlet reads: "Dear High School Graduate ... Now it's time to make the rest of your dreams come true. The Air Force can help. "We offer outstanding job and leadership training, a variety of programs to help you pay for college expenses, plus the free time you'll need to pursue your interests." Another Air Force pamphlet reads, "Whether you are undecided how to go about achieving your goals or already have a plan, one thing's for sure: The Air Force Reserve will assist you in creating a life above and beyond."

Other than the seemingly paradoxical insinuation that one "creates" life by joining a military service, the literature goes on to list the following rewards for those who enroll: competitive pay; opportunity to travel; retirement program; leadership experience; camaraderie; and use of base facilities, including tax-free shopping privileges, golfing, bowling and more. Meanwhile a Navy pamphlet lists that service's benefits as being "good pay, regular promotions when you qualify, opportunities for advanced education through the Montgomery GI Bill, Navy Tuition Assistance, and Navy College Programs, health care and low-cost life insurance. All this and the opportunity to travel to places such as Italy, Spain, Hawaii, and Japan just to mention a few." All this is said without the hint of the danger that awaits one who joins a group of working warriors. With bright literature, smiling faces on each page, donning a "why not join in the fun" demeanor, one can only wonder, why aren't we all in the Army? It not only pays for the education any free man deserves, it also pays you to go have fun in Hawaii.

This imagery draws comparison to beautiful women frolicking on the beach, who stop to take notice of an extra "cool" guy draining some nicotine down his pipes. That literature, in essence, is the image of a prototype of cool so many men attempt to achieve—that venerable rustic look of the Marlboro man. But like military literature leaving out images of dead bodies, we don't see the real Marlboro man suffering from cancer. And although more solemn, the Marines pamphlet is laudatory as well, praying upon the adventure factor present in young adults. "There is a world out there that you have only heard about. It is a world where heroes are made and missions are accomplished." Still, there is no talk about the factor of death.

A bit unsettling, nearly each piece of literature speaks directly to high school students. "High school seniors can begin taking part in the Marine Reserve before graduation," reads one pamphlet. "You can work with your future reserve unit one weekend a month for up to twelve months, receiving four days pay for each weekend of service. Following graduation, you will go through recruit skills training to become a Marine Reservist."

John P. Boyce, Jr., public affairs specialist of the U.S. Army Public Affairs, Community Relations & Outreach Division in Washington, D.C., said the Army's literature does tell the real story of service. "Our literature, commercials and web information," he said, "show real recruits struggling with basic training, facing their personal challenges, working as team members and facing life's personal obstacles with the Army's values."

But when it comes to expressing the dangers of participating in the Army, Boyce feels there is nothing the Army can say about the perils people aren't already aware of. "If they've ever seen a war movie, read a book about battle or seen a newscast about any war in the past 100 years, yes … recruits are aware of the potential dangers as well as the benefits of fighting to defend our society."

When I asked Mr. Boyce to what extent recruiters discuss the dangers of being involved in the military, he said recruiters do not necessarily explain the horrors of war. "Recruiters answer recruit's questions," said Boyce. "Recruits who do go on to military service also receive a healthy dose of military history, safety training and work in teams to anticipate and avoid most dangers. This is a vital part of our culture, along with our values."

Yet the question remains—is it too little too late? Should the military do more to warn impressionable recruits about the serious presence of danger and the potential death that awaits them? Do young recruits really understand that possibility? College professor Sam Mason, an expert in psychopathology and psychology who is using an alias to protect his identity, says that young people up to 19 have not fully developed enough to understand the consequences of enrollment in the services. "Prior to [military service], it doesn't exist, but once you're into the system then it becomes sort of a gung ho attitude," said Mason. "There is no way to understand the whole grasp of [the dangers of potential service in war], it's too much first off. Developmentally their whole cognition is not even finished developing. You give a 17- or 18-year-old a gun, he might shake his head yes but I don't think he can fully understand the situation."

Mason also pointed out that in instances where people sign up for weekend service, many are caught off guard when actually called into full service. "All these reservists that have been called up, one weekend a month, two weekends a year, did you ever think you'd be called up for war, [many are asking] 'what do you mean I have to go to war.' I believe a lot of people were shell shocked they had to go to war [during the Gulf War and now once more]."

Furthermore, Mason, who served in the military during Vietnam, explained his experience has adversely affected him in many ways he could not have imagined.

"It affected me, psychologically, emotionally, physically," he said. "It still affects me. You just can't push the button in the brain then erase it. The memories are there. I choose to live with it, but that's the cost I guess, and no one knows it before going into it."

In a country where most of the population—especially the poor—do not know what it's like to see a doctor on a regular basis or are used to earning minuscule wages offered at fast food restaurants, the benefits, in addition to the image of honor and prestige associated with serving one's country, are a barrage of pleasantries; only a fool would turn away from such a wonderful opportunity. And many, fearful of a struggling job market and a fruitless future filled with financial distress, choose to rely on the perennial economy of combat forces to provide living wages and prosperity. When the dangers of service are not addressed to the extent one would experience in getting one's driver's license (we've all seen the gory videos of fun nights on the town gone wrong) it leaves little wonder that service in the military is such a popular choice among our young people.

The more we inspect the issue, one distinct difference between tobacco companies and the armed forces becomes apparent—one comes with a warning of potential harm from the Surgeon General. There is no warning at the bottom of an Army advertisement expressing "death by machine gun fire may occur," or "may cause psychological damage as we erase prior mode of behavior replacing it with license to kill." Instead, we are shown Hollywood-produced commercials and glamorized literature that portrays a fun loving group of people getting paid to go to school, hang out together, and pursue their own interests. In fact, it is known that the military spends at least 100 million dollars to produce these materials in an obvious effort to compel service, just as a company might encourage consumerism.

The military, too, is a business venture for many—American taxpayers spend more than 300 billion dollars each year on the industry that is the defense department. Though a public industry, many earn great annual salaries and the salaries of recruiters expands as the number of recruits increases. And just like smokers don't start smoking to enjoy its addictive properties or experience cancer as a result, recruits don't join the military to participate in combat. It's the image of smokers and valiant, impenetrable soldiers seen on TV that people are sold on. In an article written by Robert Hey, then-new recruit Shanan Burns is quoted as saying, "It sounds good to be a part of the world's greatest army." ("Military recruiters new message," *The Christian Science Monitor*, July 9, 2001)

For many, the Army sounds like a good idea, until they're actually deployed into open warfare. According to other professionals, many recruits are not seeking experience in combat or the ways of warriors, they're just trying to pad their resumé or pay off debts.

In the aforementioned article by Robert Hey, Norfolk, Va., Army recruiter Sgt. Marcus Campbell was quoted saying, "We've been seeing an influx of college-orientated applicants who want their college loans paid off, [or] who want money for college, who're looking to make themselves marketable."

While recruits seem to be guaranteed the best possible training from the greatest Army ever assembled, the question remains: do people know what they're getting into after reading literature and watching commercials that narrate, "If someone wrote a book about your life, would anyone want to read it," as one now on TV asks? Mr. Boyce again reiterated that the U.S. military does, in fact, do all it can possibly do to ensure the health, training and safety of recruits after they've joined. He also said that the risks of service are well documented and known throughout the country. "As with fire-fighters, policemen and other professions, the risks of injury and death are well publicized in our society and well known throughout our nation's history. We address these legitimate fears by placing a high value on our soldiers' lives, being risk averse to risking lives, planning precision military operations and, most importantly, training our people well," said Boyce.

So while it has become obvious to Americans that smoking harms the lungs, among other parts of the body, our justice department has held to the enlightened perspective that those peddlers of this product must accept responsibility for the manner in which they identify their product. Our juries and judges have scrutinized the methods by which advertisers achieve the goal of snatching up willing patrons and participants. Time and time again, these very institutions have questioned the professional ethics that tobacco CEO's continuously overlook, opting to concentrate on the benefits of smoking (e.g. the image, taste, positive affect) while avoiding the health risks until it was too late for so very many.

Whereas the tobacco companies are phasing out their use of billboards and advertising in sports stadiums, the U.S. Army has phased in sponsorship campaigns such as NASCAR stock cars and Arena League football jerseys. In the article mentioned earlier of the new message of the military, Brig. Gen. Duane Deal, commander of Air Force Recruiting Services, put it into perspective in saying, "We're on billboards. In Syracuse, New York we're even on milk cartons." The new military image is a calculated attempt to encourage independent, thrill-seeking personalities to join a club that will pay for college, travel across the world, and an annual salary, not to mention free room and board. For many, this slanted campaign leaves much unsaid and allows silence to elucidate the most devastating of all physical disabilities, death.

Syndicated columnist Norman Solomon reviewed much of the "army of one's" recruitment materials. ("Media Sizzle for an Army of Fun" August/September 2002, IMPACT press) He explains that simply by calling the Army's 800 number, one can receive a free Army T-shirt and a video called "212 Ways to be a Soldier." The article describes the video as "graphics flash with a cutting edge look (supplied by a designer who gained ad-biz acclaim for working on a smash Nike commercial)." The article adds, "There's no talk of risk and scarcely a mention of killing." The military would seem to be serving impressionable thrill seekers loads of fun without the danger.

In the video, soldiers hail the promise of college education and exciting careers as important benefits, according to Solomon. The U.S. military has even released a video game, once again putting a fantasy spin on the realities of training for and fighting wars.

Like any corporation, the military seems to have set its sights on growing. Organizations like the ROTC at high schools and colleges are not uncommon and are expanding. Recruiters are now even given access to public high school students without the permission of parents, so that they may pursue individuals thought to be good candidates for service.

But the question is not whether the military is good or bad, necessary or superfluous. The question is, are they liable for the deaths of those tantalized by a glorious, seemingly fun environment in the armed forces? Should parents, wives and children have the right to sue the Army for the loss of their loved ones? Mr. Boyce believes the Army is responsible for those soldiers that serve the institution. He says they have done and continue to do their best to ensure the well being of their personnel. "The Armed Forces protect their people," he said, "mitigate risks, provide rigorous, realistic training and serve at the direction of the president and the American people. Our government, in fact, does assist with soldiers group life insurance, casualty assistance and family benefits ... but we work far harder to avoid deaths. So, yes, our government and our society is liable in many profound aspects for the deaths of military personnel ... and has been for 227 years. America honors those brave souls each Memorial Day and recognizes the living each Veterans Day."

But the question remains—would 70 million Americans be enrolled in the service if they believed their lives were at risk? Would they think twice before joining if advertising were forced to include an explicit warning that soldiers may die, and show the number of military casualties including deaths, and resulting cases of debilitation and mental-illness? Because, while it's obvious cigarettes cause cancer, one must ask if the intent of advertising weren't coercive, why would companies spend millions to make the perfect commercial? Why would the U.S. military? And if people were so interested in being a soldier, why is it necessary to spend so much time, effort and money engaging them?

The mediums in use seem to be specifically designed to garner the interests of a young video game playing, thrill-seeking generation. Simply put, advertising sells products. Or does it simply inform? Mr. Boyce said the military's goal is to use the means at its disposal and let Americans know what the Army today is about. "Our goal is to show people what it's like to be in the Army today using many different media to meet their information needs and desires. It's

choice to serve our nation freely."

Still, one must consider that most Americans know cigarettes are bad for them and can cause death. Yet tobacco companies are forced to label their products as harmful and are not allowed to advertise anywhere near schools where children attend. So while Americans may very well recall the deaths of Vietnam, it might take a reminder, a warning label on the beautifully packaged career in the military, to enlighten recruits (especially those who weren't around to endure a fiasco like Vietnam) of the horrors TV and books can never properly depict.

Each American deserves the right and privilege to serve our great nation, but each should also be fully aware of the perils that can hardly be imagined, should one engage the enemy in open warfare. One should be told of the apocalyptic nature of war, where each second survived is but a fleeting blessing from a hell unimaginable. Just take a look at the photojournalists who documented the last Gulf War, the charred bodies of civilians and soldiers, who once were civilians like many of our young people, and who just happened to be wearing fatigues in hopes of bettering their lives and the lives of their families.

—Originally published in the April-May 2003 issue of IMPACT press; reprinted on several websites including Utne.com, in the September 19, 2003 issue of the site's "Web watch."

AMERICA: HOME OF THE HATEFUL

>I<

There is little doubt that Planet Earth, as we know it, is being hurled into a new abyss of barrenness, as mankind leaves a path of pollution and destruction to mark its advances. But of all our planet's resources, the one that is most steadily being depleted is not some mineral, or even the rain forest. No. Love–humanity, patience, tolerance–is the substance most endangered on Earth.

No better proof of such a sorrowful reality exists than the recent outcry of opposition to gay marriage, as expressed by politicians and, in particular, the American people. Many, of whom a great number were never moved by the spirit of peace to protest the war or sexism, have teemed onto the streets across the U.S. to castigate homosexuals. In fact, according to a Time/CNN poll conducted in early February 2004, 62 percent of the population "oppose legalization of same-sex marriages; less than a third favor it."

And as history is fated to repeat itself, lawmakers and politicians, embroiled in the debate over gay and lesbian rights of today, sound a lot like the lawmakers and politicians who strongly resisted the 1960s Civil Rights movement. At the time, many leaders cited such fears as the deterioration of the family through a mixing (both socially and sexually) of the races. And now today, many leaders are once again stating concerns that the American family is being threatened, this time by homosexuality.

Actually, the plight of both movements share a similitude that can hardly be extracted from one another: today, gays and lesbians struggle to obtain a civil legitimacy and a sense of freedom that is superior to the condescending idea that "separate" is "equal." Yet where minorities like African Americans, as well as Hispanics and Native Americans, have at least partly been successful in defeating stigmas, overturning discriminatory laws, and quieting racist rhetoric from politicians, the new preoccupation of legal intolerance concerns sexual preferences. Proof of such is witnessed in the June 2003 Supreme Court ruling (*Grutter v. Bollinger*) in favor of permitting the use of race as a determining factor in the college admissions process. Though affirmative action remains controversial, political correctness censors the type of boastful opposition that gay and lesbian marriage has garnered.

For instance, while an African American has the freedom to become a Boy Scout troop leader and participate fully, such is often not the case for the stigmatized homosexual. In fact, three years ago the Supreme Court issued a 5-4 vote that "ruled it unconstitutional for a New Jersey judge to force the Boy Scouts to accept a gay rights activist as a scoutmaster." But it doesn't end there; gays and lesbians have had to endure a mounting prejudice that is not limited to hateful subcultures, but instead extends deep into the courts of law.

Although some might say the Supreme Court's latest ruling in the case of *Lawrence v. Texas*, in which the majority ruled in favor of the plaintiff that laws should not regulate the private sexual affairs of consenting adults, expresses sympathy equivalent to that of the recent affirmative action case, the disparity between the two is proven by the malevolent words of the court's three dissenters in the Texas case. "The court has taken sides in the culture war," wrote Antonin Scalia, President George Bush's self-proclaimed favorite Supreme Court justice, on behalf of the three. Scalia went on to complain, "This reasoning leaves on pretty shaky grounds state laws limiting marriage to opposite-sex couples." Scalia wrote, "The ruling also threatens laws banning bestiality, bigamy and incest." Encompassing the three justices' stringent disagreement with the courts majority ruling, Scalia also warned that the court "has largely signed on to the so-called homosexual agenda."

Not in decades has a particular group of people been identified with such terse, sweeping language, which essentially implies that the behavior of gays and lesbians is equivalent to that of barbarism and immorality. And still, such potent, derogatory statements from conservatives like Scalia are far from uncommon. Many politicians, lawmakers and justices around the nation have based their discriminatory bent on the supposed proof that homosexuality is an extreme perversion against nature. But such a view totally ignores the consensus of the scientific community.

For instance, the American Psychiatric Association removed homosexuality from its official list of mental disorders in 1973. So obvious is the conclusion that homosexual behavior is not fully contradictory to the accord of nature, Qazi Rahman, a lecturer in the School of Psychology at the University of East London, recently authored a study that links sexual orientation with inborn characteristics. In response to what many believed was a startling discovery, Rahman was quick to remind, "We have several decades of research which suggests rather strongly that human sexual orientation is to some degree biologically determined" ("Startling Study Says People May Be Born Gay," *HealthDay Reporter*, October 6, 2003). So, while Scalia accuses his fellow judges of joining the "homosexual agenda," it appears, conversely, that conservatives like Scalia have simply signed onto a doctrinaire "anti-homosexual" agenda.

Furthermore, while Christian fundamentalists find gay and lesbian attempts at becoming adoptive parents contentious, organizations like The American Academy of Pediatrics (AAP) have taken stances that do not oppose such parental relations. Actually, the AAP issued a policy statement in the February 2002 issue of *Pediatrics* affirming, "A growing body of scientific literature demonstrates that children who grow up with one or two gay and/or lesbian parents fare as well in emotional, cognitive, social, and sexual functioning as do children whose parents are heterosexual."

Nevertheless, countless leaders in the U.S. continue to rail against what they believe is a destructive agenda to promote acceptance of homosexuality, and instances of prejudiced, anti-homosexual rulings abound.

In *A People's History of the United States*, author Howard Zinn points out that Justices Ruth Bader Ginsburg and Stephen Breyer "voted with the most conservative judges on the Court to uphold the 'constitutional right' of Boston's St. Patrick's Day parade organizers to exclude gay marchers."

Another example of outright gay-bashing occurred in February 2002, when Alabama Supreme Court Chief Justice Roy Moore cited a mother's lesbianism as grounds for denying the woman custody of her children, writing

> "...the homosexual conduct of a parent–conduct involving a sexual relationship between two persons of the same gender–creates a strong presumption of unfitness that alone is sufficient justification for denying that parent custody of his or her own children or prohibiting the adoption of the children of others... Homosexual conduct is, and has been, considered abhorrent, immoral, detestable, a crime against nature, and a violation of the laws of nature and of nature's God upon which this Nation and our laws are predicated. Such conduct violates both the criminal and civil laws of this State and is destructive to a basic building block of society–the family... It is an inherent evil against which children must be protected."

Moreover, U.S. Senator Jesse Helms made his belief that gays are inferior crystal clear when he said, "These people are intellectually dishonest in just about everything they do or say... They start by pretending that it is just another form of love. It's sickening." ("'Dear' documentary takes less-than-loving look at Sen. Helms," *Boston Herald* quoting *Congressional Quarterly*, July 9, 1998). While today's politically correct environment makes it clear that racial bigotry is unacceptable, it seems the advances of the African American civil rights movement has thrown open the valve of American animosity in the direction of the gay and lesbian movement. Yet, as freedom often provides many with complacency, instead of realizing the parallel between the African American struggle for equality and the current plight of homosexuals, Americans of today are taking up their once bemoaned heritage of prejudice– except, this time around, the discrimination is being perpetrated by all races.

In an example of the ubiquitous disdain for homosexuals, the Associated Press (AP) reported in 2002 that a coalition of several organizations used the legacy of Martin Luther King to encourage voters to repeal Miami-Dade County's gay rights ordinance. According to AP, the group made a reproachful pamphlet complete with the sponsoring effigy of King and the words: "Martin Luther King Jr. would be OUTRAGED! If he knew homosexual extremists were abusing the civil rights movement to get special rights based on their sexual behavior" ("Group's Usage of MLK's Image A Point of Debate," Associated Press, January 19, 2003).

Sadly, such an instance is not at all isolated, nor is the opinion held by those Miami-Dade County protesters who opposed the distribution of rights to homosexuals in the county. Groups everywhere, like the Washington, D.C.-based organization Family Research Counsel, work arduously not only to purport the idea that HIV is vastly a homosexual disease, but also to propagate the ill-founded notion that gays and lesbians are unfit for parenthood. In actuality, according to an ACLU fact sheet, "Not a single study has found the children of lesbian or gay parents to be disadvantaged because of their parents' sexual orientation."

Nevertheless, on January 28, 2004, the 11th U.S. Circuit Court of Appeals ruled against four gay foster parents who were attempting to adopt children in their care, upholding Florida's right to continue its absolute ban on gay and lesbian adoptions.

In spite of the wide-ranging disapproval and sometimes blatant intolerance of many Americans towards homosexuals, many have taken the less popular stand–of favoring gay and lesbian marriage rights. In an instance of bold defiance, San Francisco Mayor Gavin Newsom ignored Proposition 22, whereby the state of California refused to acknowledge same-sex marriages, when he announced that the city would begin issuing marriage licenses. In just a few days after the proclamation, which occurred in February 2004, nearly 3,000 same-sex couples had come to obtain a license–some coming as far away as New York, Georgia, Minnesota, Pennsylvania and South Carolina. While many groups quickly rebuked the illegality of the Mayor's decision to offer the licenses, others felt that the spirit of Newsom's civil disobedience was an inspiring throwback to that of Martin Luther King's own actions.

Regardless of the legality of Newsom's decision, it has, if nothing else, provoked a deluge of news coverage, acquainting the television-watching masses with the earnest excitement of gays and lesbians, suffering all-nighters in waiting for a chance to receive a license, as they attempt to solidify their love in matrimony–a freedom so many Americans take for granted.

Nevertheless, many believe that the plight of gays and lesbians is overstated; but nothing could be further from the truth. In addition to bringing the issue of marriage to dinner tables everywhere, the jovial scenes in San Francisco have also unveiled a sad state of American liberty: same-sex couples are everywhere, yet one has to look hard to notice, because gays and lesbians, more often than not, dare not engage in any public display of affection, including holding hands. While they are afforded the same basic rights as all Americans, the reality is that they necessarily live discreet lives, ever careful to tiptoe around questions concerning a "significant" other.

Theirs is a furtive subjugation. But in many ways, it is drastically obvious. Take, for instance, the comments made by U.S. Senator Trent Lott just four months before 21-year-old gay college student Matthew Shepard was brutally beaten, tied to a fence and left to die in Laramie, Wyoming. On June 15, 1998, AP quoted Lott as having said of homosexuals "You should try to show them a way to deal with that problem, just like alcohol... or sex addiction... or kleptomaniacs." Unlike his less insidious remarks concerning how great life in America would have been if Strom Thurmond and his ticket of segregation had been elected long ago, Lott never lost clout in his party for his anti-gay remarks.

Instead, such a position on homosexuality has only spread like wildfire and continues to blaze through the Republican Party. For instance, an AP interview with Pennsylvania Sen. Rick Santorum quoted him as having said, "If the Supreme Court says that you have the right to consensual [gay] sex within your home, then you have the right to bigamy, you have the right to polygamy, you have the right to incest, you have the right to adultery" ("Family Values Drive Pa. Sen. Santorum," Associated Press, April 21, 2003). "All of those things are antithetical to a healthy, stable, traditional family," the lawmaker told AP. "And that's sort of where we are in today's world, unfortunately. It all comes from, I would argue, this right to privacy that doesn't exist, in my opinion, in the United States Constitution."

Such rhetoric was even sanctioned by the White House, which responded to Santorum's venomous language with a laudatory response. On April 25, 2003, White House spokesman Ari Fleischer told reporters, "...the president believes that the senator is an inclusive man... The president has confidence in the senator and believes he's doing a good job as senator" ("Bush Praises Santorum As 'Inclusive Man,'" Associated Press, April 25, 2003).

Still more telling is the April 25, 2003 Reuters article "Bush Sees Embattled Santorum As 'Inclusive Man'" that stated, "Many Republicans supported [Santorum] and Senate Republican Leader Bill Frist called him 'a consistent voice for inclusion.'" No other group of Americans faces such open opposition and fanatic discrimination. Prior to the Supreme Court's June 2003 ruling (*Lawrence v. Texas*), 13 states held anti-sodomy laws, including four that specifically prohibited same-sex relations. At one time, states like Idaho, Oklahoma, Michigan, Mississippi, Louisiana, South and North Carolina carried penalties for sodomy ranging from three years to life in prison, revealing a long legacy of legalized hatred for same-sex relations.

In the *Lawrence v. Texas* case, Justice Scalia even tried to use the existence of anti-sodomy laws to thwart the plaintiff's initial argument that the "liberty" promised by the Constitution gives consent for adults to engage in the private sex acts of their choosing. Scalia argued that many states, in fact, banned sodomy. He also said, "we have to assure ourselves that that liberty was objectively deeply rooted in this nation's history and tradition." But such an argument, made by a man many believe President Bush hopes to one day nominate for chief justice, implies that if the original idea of liberty, did not expressly include freedom for African Americans, since they were enslaved at the time, then they should not be afforded freedom. Since a woman's right to vote has not a seed, let alone a deep root in our "nation's history and tradition,"should they not have been given the freedom to vote? Such reasoning fails to meet the high-hopes the founders of our nation held.

Regarding the nature of liberty, James Madison clearly said, "Liberty disdains to persecute" ("Who Are the Best Keepers of the People's Liberties?" *The National Gazette*, December 22, 1792). Although such a phrase was not included in the Constitution, one might say Madison's statement on the nature of liberty sums up the ideal our nation was designed to strive for: to ensure the freedoms of all. And while many conservative family groups scream that, should the government sanction gay and lesbian relationships, the result would infringe on their right to family, the truth is same-sex couples are the ones being deprived of the liberty Madison intended when he wrote the Constitution and the Bill of Rights.

Right here in the land of liberty, policy makers and politicians are treating humans who have a different sexual desire as second class citizens, even though modern psychology and science has proven homosexual love is not the result of a person's choice, but is as biologically driven as a heterosexual's love for another. While opponents of gay rights groups feel family values are on trial, so too are the original tenets of our nation that each person is endowed with the inalienable right to life, liberty and the pursuit of happiness.

Verifying a flood of extremism, in February 2004, President Bush broke new ground by proposing a constitutional amendment that would not only limit gay and lesbian Americans' right to happiness, but also, in essence, legalize their discrimination. Bush's call to approve a constitutional amendment banning gay marriages proposes to approve an amendment that is entirely antipathetic to the nature and history of America's most revered document, which has always sought to further the individual rights of Americans (with the exception of the Prohibition amendment, which was later repealed).

Such a zeal for repression should sound the alarms for all Americans because the threat to gay and lesbian sexual freedom is also a threat to their own. Best expressed by Martin Luther King's widow and nearest authority on her husband and his works on March 31, 1998, Coretta Scott King told those at the luncheon for Lambda Legal Defense and Education Fund, "I still hear people say that I should not be talking about the rights of lesbian and gay people and I should stick to the issue of racial justice... But I hasten to remind them that Martin Luther King Jr. said, 'Injustice anywhere is a threat to justice everywhere.'" A few years later, on November 9, 2000, while speaking at the National Gay and Lesbian Task Force's 13th annual Creating Change conference, King said, "All forms of bigotry and discrimination are equally wrong and should be opposed by right-thinking Americans everywhere." She went on to add, "I appeal to everyone who believes in Martin Luther King Jr.'s dream to make room at the table of brotherhood and sisterhood for lesbian and gay people."

But MLK's dream hasn't been realized; neither has that of our founders. Still, everywhere, momentum to restrict the rights of gays and lesbians is growing, and Americans have to begin questioning the roots of this new hatred. When popular radio therapist Dr. Laura Schlessinger openly refers to homosexual behavior as "deviant sexual behavior," we must ask ourselves, has America simply exchanged its cultural antipathy for blacks, simply to make gays and lesbians its new whipping post? What is it about hate that draws so many supporters, yet requires decades to overcome? In part, the answer may lie in our nation's arrogance.

Consider these points: President Bush tells us he went into Iraq to root out injustice. President Bush tells the American people that injustice was a trademark of Saddam Hussein's regime: women were not treated as equals, and the citizens of Iraq were subjugated to an intolerant government void of "justice." Meanwhile, in the year

2003, while Saddam's regime was being toppled and his statue drug irreverently through the streets of a "liberated" Baghdad, same-sex couples in Texas were pulling their blinds down, careful not to mutter a word of their private relations in public for fear of arrest and condemnation. While American servicemen risked–and some lost–their lives to accomplish Bush's goal of ousting an "evil" dictator and bringing democracy and justice to Iraq, gays and lesbians weren't even permitted the right to adopt one of the 43,000 children languishing in the state of Florida's foster care system.

And while those opposing the advances of the gay and lesbian rights movement have used issues like morality, the family, nature, and perfect love to aid their opposition, in a world so vacant of compassion and bona fide love, what could be more immoral than to deny a child a loving home? And what is more contrary to humanity than denying, be it constitutional or otherwise, a union between two lovers who are fully betrothed to one another? What could be more malicious, more unnatural, more unhealthy than raising children in a society that says yes to war, yes to greed, and yes to intolerance, and, yet, says no to compassion and acceptance?

When all is said and done, what act could be more deviant than squandering love, the world's most divine substance, with a message of prejudice and hate?

Alas, Americans have grown up believing themselves "liberators" and purveyors of "equality" and "justice." But the truth is America may need to liberate itself from its perpetual propensity to hate.

—*Originally published in the April-June 2004 issue of IMPACT press.*

AN INTERVIEW WITH AMY GOODMAN

⨯⊢⊂

Praised for her passionate pursuit of truth, Amy Goodman is the host and executive producer of *Democracy Now!*, an hour-long daily independent radio and television news program. On January 21, 2006, Goodman spoke on the campus of the Florida Institute of Technology, located in Brevard County, a notoriously conservative county where her show began airing at the start of the New Year. Goodman's presentation was received with great adulation by a community besieged by religious ideologues. Many in the audience were notably affected by Goodman's critique of the profound criminality of U.S. foreign policy as she explained that people around the world hold an emotionally ambivalent view of the United States, seeing U.S. power as both the sword and the shield.

Over the years Goodman has established a reputation as a demanding journalist willing to unapologetically ask tough questions of the most powerful politicians across the political spectrum. In fact, the *Washington Post* described Goodman as "the journalist as uninvited guest. You might think of the impolite question; she asks it." In recent days Goodman's program *Democracy Now!* has spent much time speaking to victims of U.S. torture and discussing the nation's long history of perfecting such techniques. Goodman has received numerous journalism awards, such as the Robert F. Kennedy Memorial Prize for Best International Radio Documentary and Best Religious Documentary from the National Catholic Association of Broadcasters. She is also the recipient of the American Humanist Association's 2005 Humanist Heroine Award.

Fifteen days before the event, on January 6, I spoke to Goodman via telephone about how independent media programs like *Democracy Now!* can affect communities nationwide.

JN: *Democracy Now! recently began airing in Brevard County, Florida, an area known for its radical right-wing conservatism. What does the fact that your program now airs in such a community say about people's desire for independent media? And how do you feel a program like yours can transform the media community, mired in the corporate political establishment?*

AG: I think that the traditional political categories are breaking down now—the distinctions between conservative and liberal, right and left. I mean conservative Republicans, like progressives, care deeply about issues of corporate control and privacy—you know, the whole controversy over spying. It's the Republicans and Democrats as well as others who are saying, "Wait a second here. Does this violate the basic values of the people of this country?"

And then of course there is what's happening in Iraq. I don't think those who are opposed to the war are a fringe minority or even a silent majority, but the silenced majority, silenced by the corporate media. And I think they run across the political spectrum. People are deeply concerned about the number of body bags coming home: casualties here, casualties there, and what is being accomplished. And that's why I think *Democracy Now!* is growing so quickly and is on a lot of public radio and television stations around the country. There's a hunger for independent voices across the political spectrum.

JN: *You mention this breakdown of clear-cut right and left politics with the issues you've just articulated, but we also have these other issues, things like affirmative action, where there is a very definitive difference of opinion. Do you feel there's room for those sides to see common ground on an issue as divisive as that?*

AG: Yes, I think there is common ground. I think it's important also just to get the voices of people at the grass roots as opposed to the small circle of pundits that we see so often on all of the networks—this small circle that knows so little about so much and that explains the world to us.

JN: *There were a lot of people at the start of the war in Iraq who had a great deal of confidence and faith in their leadership but who have now seen a breakdown in competence. Do you think by giving voice to those people, you're emboldening them to get more directly involved; showing them they can or should have a great deal of input?*

AG: I think that information is power and also hope. It's the people knowing where they stand. I think someone's political bent doesn't matter. People want to have honest information and then they can make their own decisions. And it's fine to disagree. But what's critical is to have accurate information.

JN: *In an interview for Yes! magazine you said, "It's not journalism's role to pass on opinions. It's journalism's role to get to the truth." Has this become a somewhat novel idea limited to maverick journalists like you? And how do you define the objective search for truth?*

AG: I don't think anyone can be objective. I think we can be fair and accurate and open up the space. This is our role as journalists, for people to have a debate and discussion about the most important issues of the day like war and peace, life and death. I think that's what we're striving for. I think a lot of people have a point of view. And as long as you're honest about that and you make sure that other people get their points of view heard, that's what we can do.

JN: *So the dishonesty is playing the fiddle of objectivity?*

AG: Well, there's that sense, and we'll bring you both sides. So often Democrat and Republican are not the two sides. Often they're the same side. Let's not forget it wasn't just the Republicans who paved the way for war. The Democrats joined with the Republicans in authorizing the invasion of Iraq. So it's not just the Republicans' responsibility. And I think the range of opinions spreads beyond those in power in Washington.

JN: *Do you think it makes sense for a sixty-minute radio news program to spend as much time as say, National Public Radio does, reviewing music and discussing art when things are so crazy with political corruption and so forth in our country?*

AG: Culture is so important and it is a response to what is happening in the world. And it also is a part of making the world a more livable, beautiful, and just place—that people are expressing themselves through their cultures. And I hope we bring that to it as well. I think *Democracy Now!* is a very hopeful program because it's people talking about what's going on and talking, most importantly, about what they're doing about it. And that has always been hopeful for people to know it's not just about sitting back and listening, but it's figuring out how you fit into the world and what you can do. It's hearing all the different solutions and organizations that people are involved with and how they're working together. I think that's why, no matter how difficult the issue, people find it so hopeful and why so many people and stations are picking it up right now.

JN: *Do you have a favorite smaller, independent socio-political magazine that you like to read?*

AG: We comb the Internet and newspaper stands. We talk to many, many people here and around the world in pursuing the stories that we do everyday. So I would say there's no one particular source of information. In fact I think the most important thing is to really branch out and get a diversity of views and publications, and read as much as possible. That's what the *Democracy Now!* team and its producers are doing every day, in addition to working on the shows for the next day.

JN: *Many try to write you off as a political progressive participating in activist journalism. Should activism and journalism go hand in hand?*

AG: I think it's a passion for peace and for a diversity of voices to be heard. And that's what makes America great. And that's how we can find our way and build a more just society. And there's room for everyone and we have to be tolerant and hash out the issues. I don't think there's one truth. I think it's about hearing different truths, and that's what our role is as journalists—to put those truths out there.

—*A version of this interview was originally published in the May-June 2006 issue of the Humanist magazine.*

On Saturday April 28, 2007, 1,500 Miami Dade College students participated in a graduation ceremony featuring guest speaker President Bush. Despite the *Miami Herald's* predictions that Bush would receive "more cheers than heckles," a group of people equal in size to the number of graduates greeted the president with a criminal's welcome. On the same day that activists in cities across the country took to the streets calling for the impeachment of Bush and Cheney, more than 1,000 people confronted Bush with a wall of opposition along the entryway of the Kendall, Florida campus.

In an April 27 article, "Cheers likely for Bush at MDC speech," the *Miami Herald* quoted accounting and economics teacher Maria Mari saying, "This is a commuter school. Students don't stick around" to plan protests. Yet, the number of young protestors was equal if not greater than the number of aged activists. Luis Cuevas, Florida state coordinator of the Progressive Democrats of America, was impressed by the turnout. "I think it's a wonderful experience to see so many people, particularly very young people, present at this place," he said.

First-time protestor, 25-year-old Miami resident Cassandra Wendels said the event was both positive and empowering. "This is actually my first event,"

IMPEACHMENT PROTEST, MOVEMENT, IGNORED BY CORPORATE MEDIA

⊁⊀

she said. "It's nice to feel so much energy from other people so that it makes the whole point stronger. It's nice to know you're not sitting home and watching the shit on TV that you're actually there, you're in it. I'm going to get off my couch a lot more and make a whole lot of other people get off of their couches a lot more and be here."

Responding to the *Herald's* contention that Bush was almost guaranteed a friendly welcome, Miami Beach resident Dave Patlack said he felt like protesters stood up to the paper's challenge. "This is hugely successful," he said. "The *Miami Herald* on Friday threw down the gauntlet to South Florida activists and said, show it. And we did, today. This is the largest outpouring against Bush we've had in Miami Dade County. This is a blue county and we don't want Bush here. He's a bad example for commencement. This should be a day of celebration for the students, their families, the staff, the teachers. But today we feel the pain that Bush brought to this country through his lies, through his integrity loss, through the terrors that he has brought throughout the world."

Despite the solid showing from a city often labeled politically apathetic, many news reports failed to portray the event accurately. In its online story, "Protestors Greet President Bush With Jeers," CBS 4, Miami-Ft. Lauderdale inaccurately reported that only "dozens of protestors voiced their disapproval of the President's actions in

Iraq," during Bush's commencement speech (April 28, 2007). The short article went on, "Not everyone at the protest had something bad to say about Mr. Bush. Even though they were in the minority, there were some people who had nothing but good things to say about the president's performance."

Actually, at the height of the event, around 5:00 PM, less than a half-dozen Bush supporters waded through a sea of more than 1,000 anti-Bush protestors. While the South Florida *Sun-Sentinel* had no trouble reporting that the president spoke to "1,600 of the College's 8,000 graduates," the paper demeaned the protest twice, stating, "hundreds of protestors" had gathered outside of the college. One of the event's many organizers, Simon Rose, press secretary for Democracy for America, Miami, believes inaccurate crowd estimates are unforgivable. "Before you cite a number, if you say hundreds then you better make darn sure you've counted the number of people rather than arbitrarily throwing out a number. I know several people who counted well over a thousand."

Even more important than the media's low-balling of protest attendance, Rose believes the ratio of supporters to detractors was the real story that went unreported. "What was really significant is that there were over 1,000 protestors against his policies as opposed to maybe half-a-dozen supporters," said Rose. "To me, it is almost shameful that the media isn't reporting that, the tremendous ratio of protestors versus supporters. Frankly, I expected a lot more supporters of the president to show up. I felt very good about how few did show-up, it's so telling." Among those at the event were Miami Dade College graduates, punk rock musicians performing anti-war anthems, activists with bullhorns bellowing for impeachment, college and high school students, members of the Unitarian Universialists, a couple holding helium field balloons with "Impeach" slogans, and middle aged men and women across the ethnic spectrum.

Brad Shaw, an African-American from Miami, said he came to the protest to "stop Bush and his crimes against us all…. He needs to respect us all," said Shaw, adding, "Bring our troops home, they need to come home and see their kids, they need to be back home with us." Graduate art student Jacqueline Gopie who attends Miami's Florida International University, set-up her paper-mache anti-Bush work on the side of the road. Describing the piece, Gopie said, "I have a cartoon that Jim Moran did where one hand he's bleeding Iraq, he's like 'Oh, I can't.' This is the first time he's ever enacted the veto and this is what he uses it for. So I just put all of these articles of people, the names of the dead, people who have been killed, various stories about the Iraq war and just put them all over his body to show how hypocritical it is. "It's in reaction to the statement Bush made when he signed a veto of a bill that was going to increase funding for stem-cell research," she said. "He said he didn't want to allow stem-cell research because it would mean the murdering of innocent lives."

A Gainesville resident, Cuevas, bolstered the event's impeachment theme by dressing as an imprisoned Dick Cheney. "This is part of the backbone campaign—Chaingang.org —we carry across the country to places where there are activities," he said. "And what we want to do is attract attention to the problems and to the individuals that have caused it. And at the same time to bring attention to the activities of the activists who are against the war."

Rose believes the event was an indication that Miami is a city waking from its slumber. "This was by far the largest demonstration in the county since the FTAA protest," he said. "Miami is always being accused of being apathetic and so many people turned out for this thing. That's a story in itself, that Miami is getting the message."

—Originally published under the title, "Miami Impeachment Protest," in the July-August 2007 issue of Z Magazine.

HUNDREDS OF THOUSANDS TAKE "STOP THE WAR" MESSAGE TO CONGRESS

>K

On Saturday January 27, 2007, hundreds of thousands of peace protestors responded to President Bush's call for a troop surge with a peace surge of their own that flooded the streets of Washington, DC and other cities around the U.S. These massive anti-war demonstrations took place less than a week after President George Bush urged Congressional support for an additional 21,500 troops for the war in Iraq. Veterans, labor and religious groups, and people from around the U.S. marched along a route that encircled the Capital building. While the usual controversy has ensued over attendance numbers, one thing is certain, the march route was altered to accommodate more participants than the police expected.

Crowds chanted, "No more war!" "This is what democracy looks like," "Not one more dollar." Other protestors, including many parents with their children, were perched upon government buildings along the march route, brandishing home-made signs calling for

world peace and a quick end to military conflict. A group of Code Pink women carried a large pink slip above their heads chanting, "Here come the pink slips."

Florida Peace activists Vicki Impoco, Sharan Miller, and Mindy Stone marched with a banner reading: "Melbourne, Florida, War Isn't Working, Troops Out Now!" Impoco, who is the co-organizer of Brevard Patriots for Peace, said she flew to Washington to try and put a stop to the president's plans for escalation in Iraq. Impoco was particularly encouraged to see so many veterans at the event: "I think what moved me the most was when I saw a Marine in full dress just walking through the crowd," she said. "I went up to him and shook his hand and thanked him for his courage and for being there." She was also surprised with the tone of the march. "That was my first demonstration in Washington and I was really overwhelmed by the number of people that were there and how peaceful it was and how everyone just bonded." A long-time activist with several DC marches under her belt, Sharon Miller said there were more young people involved than in the past. "I think the difference was the families and the college students, especially the high school students. I think that was a huge difference from past marches."

Capturing the mood of the event and its participants, Rev. Graylin Hagler of Plymouth Congregational Church, Washington, DC said he wanted to remind the Congress, "When we voted in mid-term elections...it was not a multiple choice question; when we voted it was not a suggestion; when we voted it was a directive to bring our troops home now."

A variety of groups and individuals were on hand, from 12-yearold Moriah Arnold of Harvard, Massachusetts to Rev. Jesse Jackson and Rabbi Michael Lerner, editor of *Tikkun*. Moreover, several U.S. Representatives were there with plans for peace. Speakers included: Rep. Dennis J. Kucinich (D-OH), a candidate for the 2008 presidency; Rep. John Conyers (D-MI), chair of the House Judiciary Committee; Rep. Lynn Woolsey (D-CA); Rep. Maxine Waters (D-CA); and Rep. Barbara Lee (D-CA). Woosley, joined by Waters and Lee, has introduced HR 508, "Bring Our Troops Home and Sovereignty of

Iraq Restoration Act," which she told marchers would "end the U.S. occupation in Iraq within six months, saving lives and limbs and money and American's standing in the world." Adding, "HR 508 is the only comprehensive legislation that puts us on the fast track to a fully funded military withdraw from Iraq." Rep. Waters, an African-American, offered fierce criticism of the Administration, including Condoleezza Rice. "My name is Maxine Waters and I'm not afraid of George W. Bush. My name is Maxine Waters and I'm not intimated by Dick Cheney. My name is Maxine Waters and I helped to get rid of Rumsfeld. My name is Maxine Waters and Condie Rice is nothing but another neocon and she doesn't represent me."

Throughout the event, at the foot of the stage, the anti-war group Code Pink had set-up a moving display—an eight-foot cylinder containing pairs of shoes representing the Iraqi dead. One of the group's members encouraged protestors to place an ID tag, including the victim's name, gender, age, and manner of death, onto one of the hundreds of shoes spilling out five feet around the base of the memorial.

By the protest's end, trashcans overflowed with signs and many activists headed home. Still a steady stream of sad-eyed volunteers placed tags on shoes.

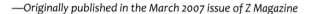

—*Originally published in the March 2007 issue of Z Magazine*

This year, five poignant and increasingly radical national protests have taken place, dating back to January 27, 2007 when nearly half a million people occupied Washington, DC. Despite the increasing number of protesters willing to be arrested, not to mention the diverse composition of the anti-war movement—including students, workers, many from the liberal elite, and soldiers— the mainstream media continues to nourish apathy and pessimism about the strength of the anti-war movement. While acknowledging the lack of support for the war, it constantly dismisses collective actions with little to no coverage, preferring to focus on every negative angle it can conjure up. The vitality of the anti-war movement and the increasing daringness and dedication of its members, however, has never been greater.

OVERVIEW OF THREE NATIONAL ANTI-WAR PROTESTS IN 2007

⨯⊀

October 27

Most recently, on October 27, 2007, about 100,000 or more people took to the streets in more than a dozen cities including Boston, New Orleans, Los Angeles, Orlando, Ft. Lauderdale, Chicago, New York City, Seattle, San Francisco, Philadelphia, Jonesborough and Chattanooga (Tennessee), Salt Lake City, Denver, Rochester, and elsewhere.

As part of the October 27 event, 2,000 to 3,000 activists from Florida and nearby southern states rallied at Lake Eola Park in Orlando. Activists browsed progressive literature tables and listened to speakers including activist and *Z Magazine* co-founder Michael Albert, Democratic presidential candidate Sen. Mike Gravel, and Florida CodePink organizer Lydia Vickers, among others. After listening to the speakers, the group took to the streets of downtown Orlando armed with signs such as "Give Me Back My Constitution," "Rich Man's War, Poor Man's Blood," and "Torture Is War Crime."

After the march, organizer Matt De Vlieger wrote in his blog: "Well, we didn't quite end the war on October 27, but we certainly strengthened our movement in the region and proved that the

Southeast has what it takes to put on a massive revolutionary one that was extremely peaceful and empowering."

The event coincided with the Florida Democratic Convention, also being held in Orlando. According to the Associated Press, the convention was attended by 3,000 people. In a show of solidarity, several convention-goers participated in the demonstration. Some, like Palm Bay resident Michele Paccione, took their uncompromising anti-war agenda back to the convention, urging fellow Democrats to become more involved in the anti-war movement. De Vlieger went on to point out the significance of an anti-war march drawing as many people as the well- funded Florida Democratic party. "Does that tell you something?" he asked.

September 29

On September 29, 2007 thousands of anti-war protesters participated in the Troops Out Now Coalition's anti-war march on Washington. The protest took specific aim at Congress, demanding that it cut off funding to the war and bring it to an end. The march was the culmination of a week-long encampment in front of Congress where protesters set up booths, erected a large billboard demanding that Congress stop funding the war, listened to musicians and speakers, and attended vigils and workshops.

During the march a segment of activists broke from the main group to take over a street around the corner from the Capitol. Participating in peaceful civil disobedience, hundreds of mostly student activists blocked an intersection. A handful of inconvenienced travelers cheered the protestors. In an attempt to ignore the disobedi-

ence, DC police blocked off area streets, making the action appear to be part of the larger march.

One of the only national stories on the event came from the *Washington Post*. The *Post's* headline read, "War Protest Draws Small Crowd: Participants Cite Public Apathy in Low Turnout for Rally at the Capitol." The paper reported that "hundreds" turned out for the event, a gross underestimation. The focus of the piece was on the inability of the anti-war movement to generate support: "Several rally goers acknowledged that the size of the rally illustrated how difficult it is to get people in the United States to become activists, even though a majority of the public opposes the war, according to polls."

(*Photo by Joseph Nall*)

September 15

On September 15, 2007 between 50,000 and 100,000 people participated in an anti-war march sponsored by the ANSWER coalition. A large turnout by veterans and veteran families, as well as mass civil disobedience, signaled a turning point for the anti-war movement. Early in the afternoon participants streamed into Lafayette Park. Ken Hudson from Miami, Florida was among those who gathered at the park to hear the slate of speakers. Hudson, his son Jeffrey, and friend Christina all wore T-shirts mourning the loss of Iraq war veteran Christopher Hudson. "We're here to protest the war," said Hudson. "My little brother got killed over there three years ago. We just think it's senseless.... I was never political, ever. And then this happened to Chris.... We got really involved."

Among the speakers who most successfully stirred the crowd was Rev. Lennox Yearwood. Yearwood told the rally-goers that war and racism are obsolete and said, "The revolution may not be televised, but it will be uploaded." Yearwood also referred to an unprovoked arrest by Capitol police that sent him to the hospital just days earlier on September 10 during the General Patreaus hearings. Video of the incident shows Yearwood being removed from the line without explanation. When he objected and attempted to keep his place, officers pulled Yearwood to the ground. In his speech at the protest Yearwood, a former officer in the U.S. Air Force Reserve, said that it was ironic that he was lying in the halls of Congress while another

officer was lying to Congress. Video showed the police demanding that Yearwood, held down under the weight of several officers, stop resisting arrest. "Here I am just laying there and they're like, 'stop resisting,' I'm like, 'I'm not resisting. What are you talking about?'"

Activist Cindy Sheehan, in an interview after her speech, said the protest signified the American people's refusal to buy pro-war government propaganda. "I think it's so important and I think it shows there are so many people here in this country who aren't buying the lies anymore, if they ever did buy the lies." Sheehan said she plans to look at the bigger picture when she runs for election against Nancy Pelosi (D-CA) in the next election. "I think the unfettered crony capitalism we have is a major part of the problem, if not the problem. So that's what my candidacy is going to challenge."

Rev. Graylan Hagler, president of Ministers for Racial, Social and Economic Justice, echoed Sheehan's concern for United States policy beyond the current Iraq war. "It's up to us to bring an end to this war; to bring an end to the kind of adventurism that continues this war; to bring an end to the kind of colonialism and neocolonialism that is really the foundation of adventures like this; and to really begin to try to rebalance the country in an equation of justice." Other speakers included Ralph Nader, former U.S. Attorney General Ramsey Clark, Adam Kokesh of Iraq Veterans Against the War, Medea Benjamin of Code Pink, and Gloria La Riva from the National Committee To Free the Cuban Five. Before the last speech had ended, people began pouring onto Pennsylvania Avenue. Numerous choruses erupted, chanting: "This is what democracy looks like," "Impeach Bush," "Support the troops, bring them home," "1, 2, 3, 4, we don't want your fucking war."

At the end of the permitted march route several thousand pro-testers took over the grounds surrounding the Capitol building. Activists of all ages climbed over the fencing that usually funnels traffic

down the Capitol's cement sidewalk. At least 5,000 people swarmed both the cement walkway and the grassy surrounding area to participate in a die-in to represent lives lost in Iraq. Realizing where the stream of people had led, some protesters left, but many remained, despite uncertainty about whether police would be making arrests. Protester Brendan O'Connor said he hadn't planned on participating in the die-in, "It just sort of happened. We just kind of fell in with it. We're here to show a presence, to add more people." Adorning a camouflage jacket and sunglasses, New Yorker Zach Hasychak reclined on his elbows, facing the Capitol. "Something needs to be done and nobody else is doing it," he said. "I'm definitely willing to get arrested." Protesters chanted: "Our house, our house, our house, our house."

In one of the more iconic examples of civil disobedience, a man stepped onto a barricade and shouted, "What do we want?" to which those behind him replied, "Peace." Thrusting a sign that read "Support the troops, bring them home," he called out: "When do we want it?" "Now," they shouted. Wearing a pink crown and looking something like a 21st century Christ, the man jumped into a group of swarming officers. It took four of them to wrestle him to the ground. Still he held his sign and called out, "What do we want?" Even when they ripped the sign from his grip and put a knee in his back, his voice persisted: "When do we want it?" "Peace... now," replied his fellow protesters. A subset of marchers scolded the police, chanting: "The whole world is watching, the whole world is watching." He was one of 190 or so nonviolent anti-war activists who were arrested.

Despite its failure to report on the size of the march, the New York Times nevertheless wrote that the demonstration "evoked the angry spirit of the Vietnam era protests of more than three decades ago" ("Anti-war Protest Ends with Dozens of Arrests," September 16, 2007). The AP noted that the number of people committing civil disobedience outweighed previous Iraq war protests.

While many gauge the success of Washington demonstrations by their size, Chris Banks, an ANSWER organizer, said, "I think the size of demonstrations is one way to measure its impact, but it's not the only way and it's not even the most accurate way. This demonstration, like the demonstration on March 17 at the Pentagon, was a very important step in the anti-war movement because these two demonstrations had enormous participation from veterans, veteran families, and active-duty soldiers. On March 17 they were about a third of the entire demonstration and in this demonstration they led the march the whole day. It speaks to a growing resistance within the military. The military resisters are one of the most important anti-war forces."

Banks felt that the arrest of Iraq war veterans and the treatment of citizens at the protest are telling of the way in which the Administration views soldiers and democracy. "For everybody here who had the experience of seeing how the troops are speaking out as veterans and soldiers are then arrested and treated like criminals…. It's a good experience here for everybody to see that."

Two days before the Washington demonstration, NPR's "Talk of the Nation" did a segment titled, "War Opposition Fails to Gel for Antiwar Movement." The story questioned the effectiveness of the movement to end the war. Of course, NPR failed to broadcast live or in-depth coverage of the September 15 march. The only coverage it offered was in a separate story which featured just two short quotes

from activists and demeaned the size and magnitude of the event by reporting just "several thousand" demonstrators had participated.

While the mainstream media took every opportunity to inundate its audience with the pro-war voice of General Petraeus during the much anticipated hearings on Capitol Hill, when it came to a mass anti-war march on the Capitol, it was business as usual. *USA Today*, for instance, went so far as to run an Associated Press story that "several thousand" were in attendance, but decided to omit a line later in the piece that relayed "tens of thousands of people" appeared to be in attendance ("Scores arrested at Iraq war protest," September 16, 2007).

Despite the mainstream media's lack of coverage of the event, activists have utilized YouTube, photo sharing sites, myspace, and more to widely publicize the events. Protesters have realized that national marches are acts of defiant revolt. As protesters chanted on September 29, "If they won't give us peace, we'll take it...." Americans are giving up polite chants for militant demands.

—*Originally published in the January 2008 issue of* Z *magazine.*

WHY WE MUST BE RADICALLY COMMITTED TO PEACE: THE GREATER PURPOSE OF THE CURRENT ANTI-WAR MOVEMENT

⨝⫟

With 72 percent of the troops believing that we should withdraw within 12 months, the continual battery of horrific developments in Iraq, and the continual pressure of anti-war activists around the nation, the pro-war mongers are now stuttering with dead words.

On March 18th 2006, about 300 people took to the streets of the mostly conservative community of Melbourne, Florida. For the first time, we matched our passion for peace with a willingness to amplify our message. Just an hour shy of the St. Patty's Day parade, we nonviolently bombarded the jovial Saturday afternoon affair with the horrible reality both our troops and the Iraqis experience daily. A steady stream of anti-war activists, armed with signs such as 'surfers for peace,' 'end the war now,' 'no wars in my and my grandson's name,' as well as 99 headstones mourning the deaths of Florida soldiers flooded the narrow sidewalk overflowing with unsuspecting St. Patty's event goers. As some began to call out the usual rhetoric — "the troops are fighting for your freedom" or "you're not supporting the troops" — we chanted "1,2,3,4 we don't want your bloody war" and "bring the national guard back to the nation" and "what do we want, peace; when do we want it, now." The local paper, *Florida Today*, described the march: "Looking like a mile-long walking graveyard, nearly 200 Iraq war protesters marched slowly, but loudly, from Front Street to City Hall...." While the paper was wrong about our size, most agree we had much closer to 300, the paper was nonetheless right about one thing, we were loud. And that loudness, which was heard by the *Associated Press* ("Florida Groups Gather To Protest Third Anniversary Of Iraq War") and local TV stations covering the event, kicks off a new commitment to ending our cordial passivity. Polite protests are over. The time has come to get (nonviolently) radical, to realize the broader duty of the peace and justice movement. We have a duty to take back the moral discourse from the ideologues that have monopolized and molested it.

On March 18th 2006 I gave the following speech, which directly addressed this issue, to my fellow protestors.

>-<

More than three years ago a small group of us started the antiwar effort here in Brevard at a coffee house in downtown Melbourne. Most of us were green when it came to activism but we determined to fight the rush to war. We all hoped we could stop it. And so hundreds upon hundreds of us poured onto the streets in February and then in March in two separate dramatic demonstrations at this very same place (Melbourne City Hall). We were energized we were hopeful but in the end most of us were devastated. Despite our amazing efforts, the war began.

In 2004, I talked to a famous musician who sings for a world renowned heavy metal band, System of a Down—while many of you might not appreciate their music the group is very political and very progressive. Serj told me, having participated in the massive antiwar demonstrations and seeing the world scream out no to war, he too was let down when we went to war anyhow and that it all made him skeptical. But he also said, "... in some ways it made me more determined." And that's how I feel today. More determined and more aware that the war in Iraq is just a symptom of what's being done in our name, what the United States has come to be known for.

I think most of us realize the consequences of this war. It may cost us one to two trillions. It has already cost us more than 2,300 women and men in uniform, more than 16,000 seriously injured, thousands more adversely affected psychologically; as many as 100,000 Iraqis dead including tens of thousands of civilians, children like my two-year-old daughter who were murdered mostly by Rumsfeld's precision guided bombing of Baghdad. We all know about the lies and the oil interests. But it's time we turn our feelings of impotence and skepticism into a blistering dig to the bottom of this heap of money, flesh, oil and blood; this mound of immorality and monetary debauchery. It's time we realize that the war in Iraq is symptomatic of our nation's ethical decline, decline in Constitutional values by which I mean a respect for freedom of speech, democracy and the duties of a citizen in participating in the democratic process.

We're bombarded by corporate media distortions. We hear about Martin Luther King but never a word about his complete and utter renunciation of war in every respect; he's critique of Capitalism's thingification of human beings; we hear about Coretta Scott King but not about her defense of gay and lesbian rights; as Amy Goodman pointed out we hear about Rosa Parks but never about her trouble making activism. We hear about evil doers across the globe and the threat of terrorism but we don't hear about the 100,000 Americans who die every year due to inadequate health care so the sickeningly wealthy can own hundred-thousand dollar cars and multi-million dollar mansions. What I'm talking about is class war-faire, about American workers being stripped of their healthcare and their pensions; about unions getting crushed by vilification in New York; about Wal-Mart choking U.S. manufacturers with impossible demands until they're forced to go to China where people make scraps for working like slaves, so they can produce absurdly cheap products for Wal-Mart consumers; I'm talking about CEOs making millions while the workers that build their company can't afford to go to the doctor. Get a better job they say and I ask, don't we need people to flip burgers, wash-cars, take care of our trash, and do the dirty jobs most of us don't want to. Then why can't we pay them living wages?

But some of you are starting to wonder, where are you going with this; you're saying, Jeff, get back to the war. But you've got to understand I'm talking about war, the war we're waging on ourselves and the world. Dr. King once said: "A nation that continues year after year to spend more money on military defense than on programs of social uplift is approaching spiritual death." To put it into perspective you have to realize that the proposed defense budget for 2007 is about 440 Billion dollars and if you add the money we'll spend on Iraq and Afghanistan you're looking at 559 billion for 2007. Folks, the federal government's total revenue was less than that just 26 years ago! Forget the ramblings of the religious right, its not women's rights and other human rights that are draining our society of its moral values, its our commitment to war and violence.

You and I, everyone of us, are spending billions to ensure businesses like ExxonMobil achieve record-breaking profits, like the 36.13 billion they earned in 2005, the greatest profit in American history, whether by increasing demand for oil by starting a war or by propping up dictatorial U.S. oil company friendly regimes around the world. The conscience of this country is being slain before our eyes. And it's sad when the great author Camus' words ring true when one of his characters in the book *The Plague* said: "we can't stir a finger in this world without the risk of bringing death to somebody." Our government is systematically trying to undermine democracy around the world while touting expansion of democracy in the middle east.

In Venezuela we've aided an attempted coup against Hugo Chavez. Chavez knows all about such things, he remembers when we helped a brutal military dictator kill the democratically elected leader of Chile in the 70s. He remembers when we supported Cuban dictator Batista in Cuba; when in the 50's president Eisenhower gave the CIA the go ahead to help overthrow democratically elected Guatemalan president, who after being elected by a huge margin set out to rectify the injustice that just two-percent of the population owned 70 percent of the land. By 1990 the U.S. backed regime had left 100,000 Guatemalans dead. Chavez knows all about the CIA's work in overthrowing governments in Iran (1953); when "in 1929

U.S. firms produced more than half of Venezuela's oil"; and in Honduras where U.S. companies supplied weapons to aid a successful 1924 coup. Not to mention the fact our government kidnapped Haitian president Aristide in 2004.

Today, 80 million of our tax dollars are funding a U.S. organization, National Endowment for Democracy (N.E.D.), that pretends to aid democratic movements when in fact its real purpose is to undermine popular democratic movements. Independent, investigative reporter Anthony Fenton says of the group: "The N.E.D. played a crucial role in fomenting the opposition to Hugo Chavez, and they did play a role in the attempted coup against him in April of 2002, and very much the same patterns we have seen develop in Haiti..." Fenton went on to say that in a rare interview he conducted with an N.E.D program officer responsible for Haiti named Fabiola Cordoba, she told him:

> that when she was in Haiti in 2002, working for one of the N.E.D.'s affiliated organizations, the National Democratic Institute, she said a lot of lines were being drawn between Haiti and Venezuela, where although 70% of the population supported Aristide, there was a very fragmented opposition. The rest of the 30% was divided between 120 different opposition groups, so the objective of the I.R.I. and the N.E.D. was to consolidate this opposition to build a viable opposition to somehow break the grip that the popular movement in Haiti had on the political environment there. And she said that Chavez – something very similar was happening in Venezuela, and of course, in 2002, the coup d'état happened there on the basis of this sort of analysis, the basis, this fear that the United States has of popular democracy and the need to subvert any attempts at consolidating popular rule and implementing policies that are in the interests of the majority poor in places like Venezuela and Haiti.
>
> ..... Now the N.E.D. program officer told me that Venezuela, Haiti, Ecuador, and Bolivia are the four top priority countries for the N.E.D. in 2006, looking ahead to 2006 and, of course, Cuba is the perennial top of that list. They're a special exception, because the Department of State earmarks a certain amount of funds for the N.E.D.'s work in Cuba. In fact, they doubled the amount of money being used to subvert revolutionary Cuba in 2005.

Of course the lies, the deceit, the fascism doesn't end there. We all know about the administration's condoning torture; its approval of disappearing people or as they put it, extraordinary rendition; and now we've even resorted to abducting wives of those we suspect, using them as leverage. But we're living this Orwellian life here in the U.S. too. Americans are being spied on. As many of you know I'm apart of the ACLU's information request of the Pentagon regarding spying records on peace activists.

People, a time has come to shake this city, this county, this state, a time has come to shake this nation from its ethical stupor; time to wake up the social conservatives on the right crying about human beings wanting to get married, about women wanting to control their bodies and say, look at the murder that's taking place in your name, look at the Constitutional rights writhing in the throes of death before you. We've got to get radical. Don't get me wrong. I'm talking non-violent radicalism. Today's radicalism is believing that peace works. And if you believe that peace works I need you to say it. Peace works! It's saying that you won't sacrifice democracy and civil rights on the altar of fear and that you'd rather die free than live in chains if that's really living at all. Being radical today means token voting every four years isn't enough. It's speaking out loudly and proudly with the full knowledge that there might be microphones under your nose; it's staring the undercover agent next to you in the eyes and saying, I ain't gonna take it anymore. It's time to stomp out greed, uproot fascism, and, in the words of Martin Luther King, America, it's time to be born again.

The time has come to tell the war mongers, the neo-liberals who are more interested in profits than people; who think the right to grotesque wealth trumps the right to healthcare; who think CEOs have the right to live off of the backs of their workers like slave masters on a plantation. I mean why is it single mothers who work 60 hours a week can't afford to take care of their children? Answer: According to the Annie E. Casey, Ford and Rockefeller foundations: "one in every five U.S. jobs pays less than a poverty-level wage for a family of four." And as a result "nearly 39 million Americans, including 20 million children, are members of 'low-income working families' — with barely enough money to cover basic needs like housing, groceries and child care...." In his own day, King concluded that "an edifice which produces beggars needs restructuring" and seriously questioned claims of private ownership of natural resources. Well you can't count me in.

The divide in this nation isn't red vs. blue, republican vs. democrat. And believe it or not we're not divided by our religion or lack thereof either. The religious right has tried to aid the neoliberals in dividing this nation so that we don't rise up united. But our nation's history has shown us that Christians and nonbelievers alike can work together. Thomas Paine who didn't believe in the divinity of Christ worked tirelessly alongside many Christians to abolish slavery. During the civil rights movement believers of all stripes and nonbelievers worked together, too. Money is the ultimate divider in this nation, uplifting the wretchedly wealthy to the status of 21st century aristocrats, while the poor both in this nation and in other nations suffer the consequences. But as Dr. King said, "don't think you have me in a bind. I'm not talking about communism. You see, communism, as he put it, forgets that life is individual. At the same time, capitalism forgets that life is social." He said what is needed is a "higher synthesis." Perhaps it was his aspiration to create that higher synthesis that ultimately got him killed. I'm here to renew the call for that higher synthesis because in my mind, that's the only way we're going to cure our nation's addiction to war and greed.

In conclusion, here's what I'm trying to say to you: be a part of a revolution of American values. Don't end the anti-war slogan with Iraq. (We know Iran is on the horizon.) Look beyond this war into our culture, walk down the toy isle at a kids store, see how we're preparing another generation for military service in the service of greed and a new kind of imperialism. As has been said many times, be the change; be the drop of water in a cup; don't just fight for immediate victory, fight for the future, something beyond you and your life. Fight for a new nation. Don't oppose the Iraq war, oppose militarism in general. Oppose selling weapons to murderers, supporting oppressive regimes around the world; plotting to undermine popularly elected leaders. And lastly, don't treat your activism like a chore. It should go down like a fresh cup of fairly traded coffee, smooth, satisfying, energizing, uplifting, refreshing. It's what we're meant to do in a democracy. It should be our first priority and our number one job. When we wake up, when we go to bed we should have the question on our minds: "how can I serve justice to bring about peace?" Remember, like a business owner who hires someone to manage his business, WE own America, the politicians have simply been hired to manage our nation. It follows that if they don't get it together, they're going to be out of a job, because we're going to take back this nation or die trying!

For those of you who say it sounds all well and good, but it can't be done, from one pessimist to another, I have a simple response. In that great work, *The Plague,* by Albert Camus, the town of Oran is overtaken by a plague pandemic that cannot be eradicated. Despite the fact that there is no cure, a man named Dr. Rieux wages a perpetual battle with the illness. When questioned about his dedication to what seemed to be a lost war, Dr. Rieux said that losing a fight offers "no reason for giving up the struggle." The point is that humans can never defeat the eternal beasts of death and plague (and they serve symbolically for man's inhumanity to man); all we have in life is the ability to "struggle," to fight for "health." Perhaps the most poignant expression of this ideal of human purpose is the magistrate's son's struggle to live. Enduring inexplicable pain, the infected child's body refuses to give up the fight for survival even when mashed "in a grotesque parody of crucifixion," or battered by convulsions, screaming fits, and beleaguered tears. The boy and Dr. Rieux answer the question, so what's the point of pursuing goals and living life if, in the end, it all amounts to a headstone and a hole in the ground for forgotten bones? Because anything less would be inane; because the meaning of life is to live as best as one can, to stand resolute in the face of the inevitability of death and the recurrence of evil and "to fight..." Camus has epitomized the notion that our task in life is much greater than merely winning or losing in battle.

As humanists, that is, people who value human life, freedom, choice, and oppose cruelty and violence, we must realize our calling to choose love and realize that this movement, for peace and justice, is the only reality we are willing to accept and embrace. Dr. King taught me this. He taught me that despite the preachers and the politicians, that it doesn't matter what your religion is or isn't, love is the key. He said:

> But I know that love is ultimately the only answer to mankind's problems.... I've seen too much hate.... I say to myself that hate is too great a burden to bear. I have decided to love. If you are seeking the highest good, I think you can find it through love. The beautiful thing is that we aren't moving wrong when we do it because John was right, God is love. He who hates does not know God. He who loves has the key that unlocks the door to the meaning of ultimately reality.

OUR RIGHT TO FREELY ASSEMBLE
AND OUR DUTY AS PATRIOTS

ϪK

Despite our First Amendment guaranteed Constitutional right to assemble, the US government is moving in the dangerous direction of undermining those rights. I am a father, a student, and a suspect. My peaceful, law-abiding protesting over the last three years, my petitioning of the government, has earned me an FBI number and, in 2004, also the label of 'suspect' by Florida's Brevard County Sheriff's Office.

The much talked about case, which had to do with the Melbourne Police Dept. and the Sheriff's office videotaping, infiltrating and spying on peaceful demonstrations such as the Counter-inauguration event I was a part of, has, as many of you now know, been rectified. Both the Melbourne Police Department and the Brevard County Sheriff's Office have pledged to respect the First Amendment. This is a victory. But this is just the first step. The time has come to reclaim Constitutional Values, to remind the people in our nation that no matter how much the flag is waved, one can not be a patriot if he or she does not first honor the First Amendment.

The problem of government infringement on the right to assemble and petition is far from solved. During the counter-inauguration demonstration which caused such a stir, the Sheriff's Office gave personal information about participants, such as their social security number, date of birth, and address to someone at Patrick Air Force Base—the Pentagon. So I joined the ACLU in filling a freedom of information act request. And since they silently refused to tell us about their monitoring of people like me and the Quakers in south Florida, in June, I joined the ACLU in attempting to sue the Pentagon for the release of information it has been gathering on peace activists.

Now, whether you're for or against the Iraq war; whether you're pro-choice or anti-choice; whether you are a liberal or a conservative, a socialist or a neo-liberal, you must realize this is a problem that robs us all of our rights as Americans.

The Patriot Act, the government's disregard for our Constitutional rights, call us to ask this most important question: has freedom finally fallen to the fatalistic tandem of fear and security? Will we let it?

We know for a fact that the FBI continues to target groups and individuals because of their politics. And I can tell you from personal experience that, standing before you as a full-time student, freelance writer, and full-time father of a 3-year-old daughter, I am not a terrorist. Yet the FBI has seen fit to lump me up with such persons because I disagree with my government.

So maybe you can understand why I am afraid that the brilliant blues of American pride are fading into the dull bruises of a nation that has lost its Constitutional soul.

With so many clamoring for the idol of security and its ominous but protective embrace against fear, the US may travel a path not unlike that prophesied by an 80 year old dystopian novel, *We*. Written by Russian author Yevgeny Zamyatin, *We* tells the story of a society, the One State, that decides the "only means of ridding man of crime is ridding him of freedom." To achieve its utopian society of perfect peace, the One State eradicates individuality, privacy, and freedom; and the citizens exalt the secret police) who monitor their every action, for "lovingly protecting" them.

As America flees the open skies of liberty for the patriarchal shelter of authoritarianism, perhaps it's only a matter of time before we turn to the transparent walls of the One State: "At all other times we live behind our transparent walls that seem woven of gleaming air—we are always visible, always washed in light. We have nothing to conceal from one another. Besides, this makes much easier the difficult and noble task of the Guardians. For who knows what might happen otherwise?"

But there is a bright side, something to remember. Our simple 36-person demonstration led to dramatic, arguably, groundbreaking changes in surveillance policy at two different policing agencies — in October 2005 the sheriffs office's agreed established that so long a rally is non-violent, information about peaceful demonstrators will no longer be kept; monitoring of such protests will henceforth require approval of senior command staff; and agents are to "avoid indiscriminate collection of information on protesters, regardless of political or other affiliation." And, importantly, we sparked a community-wide discussion on the importance of protecting the Bill of Rights and the Constitution.

Ironically, during the planning stages, I remember hearing many complain that our demonstration would be futile. Some questioned the effectiveness of protesting. But I've come to realize that futility is very often the mantra of the defeated, the spiritless. To wail of a noble action's futility is to forget that every action, regardless of its direct result, lives beyond the simple boundaries of immediate success or failure. The real objective in taking a stand should never be to merely win but rather to heed the call to live and act justly, no matter the outcome.

We must protest to remind our representatives that we, the people, rule this nation. We must protest because we must waken our slumbering fellow citizens to stand up and speak out. We must protest to say the things that the evening news will not say. We must protest because to do so is to exemplify the patriot.

With our rights under such assault, there is no room for pessimism, silence, and inaction, and our impetus to act cannot rely on the likelihood our actions will procure immediately tangible results. Without erecting a powerful spirit of unification, courage and defiance, we will never catch even a glimpse of victory. Every action we take in the name of justice is a step toward defeating injustice.

Now is the time to remind people what a real patriot is; that words and peaceful actions have achieved more than all the wars of human history; that words are as powerful if not more powerful than guns; and that everyone here is a soldier for democracy if she remembers her duty to take to the streets in dissent. If she refuses to be silenced or intimidated; if she laughs into the microphones and the wire-taps, and stares directly into the eyes of the undercover agents who seek to undercut our civil liberties. Long live Constitutional values, dissent, and the spirit of true American patriotism.

—This speech was given July 1, 2006, at a First Amendment Rally in Palm Bay, Florida

OUR BEAUTIFUL STRUGGLE: PROGRESSIVE POLITICAL ACTIVISM IN THE FACE OF FUTILITY

⤬

Being an activist is a lot like being a Liberal Arts major in college. Everyone asks what the hell you're doing and what your actions are accomplishing. (Sadly, I'm not only an activist, but also a Liberal Arts grad student.) So I've had a lot of practice answering this question. Today, I want to give you my answer because I think it's important we all know why we're spending our time out here today; and why those of you who are joining us for the first or second time should continue to come out and be a peace and justice activist.

My name is Jeff Nall and I've had the privilege and pleasure of being a part of this anti-war effort since before the Iraq war began. Since 2003 I have spent more time being an activist than I have making money. When I look back on my three years of service I'm occasioned to wonder, what exactly have I accomplished? Women are being striped of choice, our government is not only conducting illegal spying, it's sanctioned torture and forsaking Habeas Corpus. And the bloodshed in Iraq continues to stain our hearts with the life-blood of more than half-a-million people dead. So what have we accomplished? Are we winning the fight? I think this is a question many activists have asked and continue to ask themselves.

The best way I can answer the question of what peace and justice activists truly accomplish is to address what I see as the spiritual and humanistic nature of political activism in the face of futility.

It's not uncommon for people like us to comment that it's time for a victory, that we need a W, no not Bush, but a W in Win/Lose column to raise our spirits. And I know its tough, as a dear friend and fellow activist of mine puts it, walking around with our tale between our legs losing one political fight after another. Now I'm not expecting you all to agree with me but I want to suggest that, if we are to create a real movement, that is one that has principles of human rights and social justice at its core, we've got to rethink what it is to win.

When you hear people say that what we do out on the streets of our cities around the U.S. is worthless in comparison to direct political campaigning, I humbly beg to differ. What we are doing is looking at the bigger picture. And we should all be aware of that broader picture. Beyond merely electing progressive leaders who share our vision, we're trying to crack the cold seal of disenchanted, uninformed, apathetic, and sometimes uncaring neighbors. We're putting the 'people' back into government; we're putting faces to justice and we should see our roles as activists as being purposed to start a wave of consciousness, to push over our fellow humans into the light of awareness like dominoes. And it's working. I can't tell you how many times people have pulled off the side of the road to join one of our peace vigils; people who've never protested a day in their life or who haven't protested in more than a decade. Young and old.

If, for instance, the Democrats do in fact take back the Congress and maybe the Senate, I truly believe it is our anti-war movement that has helped make this possible. It is our efforts in popularizing the anti-war sentiment; our efforts chiseling away at the malicious, cold-blooded pseudo patriotic propaganda our government has beaten into the populous. We are forcing our neighbors to look beyond their party affiliation and inside themselves. We are making apolitical people realize apathy is not as blissful when the blood of more than 600,000 dead humans stains their hands.

But at the end of the day, and I know this might sound less than comforting, I think it's safe to say that any victory, like life itself, is fleeting. Heraclitus, an ancient Greek philosopher, commented that fire was the fundamental element of the world. By fire he meant change, change is the one thing we can always count on.

My point is this: the only victory we will ever know is the victory of right action and the reward of comforted conscience, restful with the knowledge we have served justice as best we could. Our ethical commitment to right action can not be burdened with wins and losses, outcomes often beyond our control.

You know the famous question, if a tree falls and no one hears it, does it fall? Well one thing is for certain, the tree, if it was human, would know, would feel the fall and the subsequent consequences. So I suggest to you that our actions, whether they are felt or respected by or even affect others is irrelevant; what you are assured of is that, if your conscience is awake to cruelty and injustice, then whether or not your tree falls toward the field of right action or the thicket of irresponsible indolence, you will know and you will have to live with the consequences. At bottom, we're faced with a conundrum everyone, whether they're winning or losing the political or social struggle today, faces: the universe is beyond our control, all we can be certain of is that we have made the most of our time on this planet to refrain from joining the armies of bigotry, hatred, and violence. Living the life of an activist, speaking out against the war and torture and for human rights, we are rewarded with a good nights rest and the knowledge that we have not averted our eyes to Icarus falling from the sky; that we have cried, we have anguished, we have fought in the face of the horrors swirling about us; that we are still human, not zealous flag-waiving machines.

This is a message we must spread because even if you are a pessimist you can not refuse the kind of salient truth the great author and philosopher Camus offered in his book, *The Plague*, a classic work interpreted as an allegory for the Nazi occupation of France; a time when men like Camus joined the resistance despite the seemingly impossible circumstances they faced. In the book Camus writes:

> All I maintain is that on this earth there are pestilences and there are victims, and it's up to us, so far as possible, not to join forces with the pestilences.

Today, we stand united against the plague of war and torture with its victims. So when you're sitting on your computer late into the night writing a seemingly insignificant letter to the editor, calling out the moral imposters who are selling war as peace; who sell lazy, unthinking servility as patriotism, or sell hate as kindness; When you spend your days off from the job that pays your bills working the job that enriches your heart and soul; when you leave your job to spend an hour on a sometimes lonely, sometimes energized street corner, you are engaged in the beautiful struggle that is life. Life itself is a struggle which will ultimately end in death — so to give in because your side isn't winning or you feel like you're accomplishing nothing is to fail to realize that all victories are fleeting; that much of social history seems cyclical and that we can't simply struggle for victory (think of victory as the bonus you're happy to receive but not necessarily counting on in your budget), but rather the fight is for peace of mind; the fight is to save the very idea of humanity, that human beings are capable of love and being humane. That is why we should all stand at our respective "Peace Corner," which is what we call our protest spot here in Melbourne, Florida, every month, to remind the passerby that even in this world's impossibly inhospitable environment of rape, torture, homicide, homelessness and war, the miracle of human love has not suffocated. A humane world is still possible.

Finally, I leave you with this thought. We, as activists, are a part of a great, rich tradition of compassionate, great-souled human beings. Like those before us, we are resting peace and justice on our shoulders because someone must do it. In one of his most rousing speeches Dr. King said: "If we wait for it to work itself out, it will never be worked out. Freedom only comes through persistent revolt, through persistent agitation, through persistently rising up against the system of evil. It never comes voluntarily. We've got to keep on keeping on in order to gain freedom." "And then because there have been, in every period, there are always those people in every period of human history who don't mind getting their necks cut off, who don't mind being persecuted and discriminated and kicked about, because they know that freedom is never given out, but it comes through the persistent and the continual agitation and revolt...."

I had revolt in mind earlier this week, on Wednesday, when I attended a demo where we protested an appearance by Dave Weldon at Wickham Park. Toward the end of the protest when we were standing near the stage where Weldon was speaking, I noticed one of his supporters pointing at our group as if to identify us as 'those people.' I realized it was easy for them to identify us as alien figures of absurdity; seemingly silly to him. So I decided I'd take the rare opportunity to actually meet my elected representative face-to-face. So with my three-year-old daughter Charlotte in one arm, as has become the custom, I walked up to Weldon, shook his hand nice and firmly and said, "I hope your conscience gets the better of you and you get our troops out of Iraq." Still shaking his hand, trying to make eye contact with his squirmy, disquieted eyes, I finished by saying, "the blood of this war is on your hands."

It was a small act of defiance. I know it won't change his policies. But I think I accomplished a few things. Firstly, I reminded Weldon what all politicians need to be reminded: they are our representatives and secondly, that we're not going to sit down and let them hide from us anymore. We're going to call and write their offices; we're going to protest their fundraisers; we're going to confront them, nose to nose, with the issues; and, come November, we're going to vote them out of office.

Timidity has run its course. Polite restraint has become a risk none of us can take. We will not be deterred because we are fighting not for victory but for humanity itself.

—This speech was delivered to over 100 protestors on October 28, 2006, at the third anniversary of the Iraq war anti-war demonstration in Melbourne, Florida.

THE STORY ONLY SHOES ARE LEFT TO TELL
AND THE WORK LEFT FOR US

⋊⋉

The day after I marched in the January 27th mass demonstration against the war in DC, I attended the Holocaust museum for the first time. Though I had but a fraction of the time one needs to take-in the gut-wrenching history of the museum's multiple levels, the experience haunted me.

One day earlier, when the anti-war march was winding down, my younger brother, Joseph, and I walked to the front of the event stage. There, Code Pink had set-up what may have been the most moving display at the protest, an eight-foot cylinder containing pairs of shoes representing the Iraqi dead, which, according to a John Hopkins report is more than 650,000.

One of the group's members encouraged protesters to place an ID tag, including the victim's name, gender, age, and manner of death, on to one of the hundreds of shoes spilling out five feet around the base of the mobile memorial. The memorialized dead were victims of everything from insurgency car-bombs to pre-invasion U.S. bombing raids.

My brother and I each took a tag and solemnly tied it to a pair of shoes. Crouched down, affixing a tag to a pair of shoes, I took time to inhale the stench of death and mourn the inane brevity of these lost-lives. I reflected on the basic fact that each of the countless pairs of shoes represented a human life, a body that once breathed the air I was then inhaling, a body suffocated of life and joy and a future. Bodies that belonged to children like eight-month-old boy Mohsen Basem Naji and the one-year-old little boy named Mahdey Abed al-Atheem, both of whom existed now as a pair of warn out, donated shoes.

You really come to terms with what an empty pair of shoes means when you visit the Holocaust museum. There, you find enormous bins filled with the belongings of slain Jews including hair, scissors, and, shoes. Of all the things I saw in that museum, it's a quote by Moishe Shulstein that stands out the most. Displayed before a sea of drab, dusty, brown shoes emptied of Jewish feet by Nazi gas chambers and execution squads, it read:

"We are the shoes, we are the last witnesses.
We are shoes from grandchildren and grandfathers,
From Prague, Paris and Amsterdam,
And because we are only made of fabric and leather
And not of blood and flesh, each one of us avoided the hellfire."

On the plane ride home to Central Florida, I listened to news reports of the President's talk of war with Iran; and Cheney having told a Newsweek reporter, "Well, I'm vice president and they're not," in response to a question about criticism coming from his own party. All I could think about were the hundreds of thousands of shoes emptied in the wake of the initial bombing of Baghdad.

Proving that the drums of war are not merely practicing, but preparing for battle, the February 19 issue of Newsweek magazine reports that "At least one former White House official contends that some Bush advisers secretly want an excuse to attack Iran. 'They intend to be as provocative as possible and make the Iranians do something [America] would be forced to retaliate for,' says Hillary Mann, the administration's former National Security Council director for Iran and Persian Gulf Affairs." Newsweek also reports that a second Navy carrier group heading for the Persian Gulf will likely be followed by a third carrier. (See "Rumors of War" Newsweek Feb. 19, 2007).

Can you hear the bombs crashing indiscriminately into Iranian family homes, the futile wail of emergency vehicle sirens struggling to save lives, religious extremists pointing to the U.S. as the true face of terror? I can hear an innocent choir of civilians singing out the famous and all too redundant ode to war, a cacophonous melody of moans, cries, and screams.

The question for each and every one of us to ask ourselves now is: will we allow our government, our military to murder more children, those not at all different from our little boys and girls, our grandchildren? Will you let them?

While I was overjoyed at the success of the January 27th antiwar event, I can't help but to be, at the same time, disappointed. You see, in April 2004 I attended the March for Women's Lives, a pro-choice march attended by more than 1 million men and women. I have to admit, I sometimes looked around at the dedicated Americans who came to Washington to stop the war, wondering, where is everyone else? Have they not yet realized that the right to live without threat of occupation and invasion is as important, as personal, as the right to choose?

If we don't force Congress to reign in our nation's Executive Branch, we may all face the day when the world asks us, why should we forgive your complicity in savaging the people of two nations in less than a decade, while abhorring the complicity of the Germans who failed to stop Hitler?

For those in our nation who have become so addicted to personal luxury and comfort, who have lost humankind's greatest virtue, the power of empathy, it may do them well to recall the millions of German civilians who died during Allied bombing campaigns. Hopefully, the United States will be cleansed of its pathological addiction to machismo, militarism, and monetary materialism in time to save its people from a similar fate.

—Originally published at TowardFreedom.com
on August 22, 2007.

STOPPING THE WAR NOW: PEACE ACTIVISTS MEET WITH PRO-WAR CONGRESSMAN

᚛

After years of protesting on the streets of Melbourne, Florida five members of the Brevard's Patriots for Peace got the opportunity on April 27th to meet with congressman Dave Weldon (FL-15) for a forty-minute meeting on the war. Comprised of a graduate student, nurse, retired teacher and artist, grandmother, and writer, our delegation sat face-to-face with one of the Iraq war's greatest proponents and grilled him.

We asked if he agreed that the Bush administration had misled our nation into the war. We asked what has been achieved in Iraq in light of the death and destruction that has befallen Iraq and the death and financial strain that our nation has endured. We asked what it would take for him to begin calling for a withdrawal our troops. We asked him if he'd support a bill which would require congressional approval for an attack on Iran.

His answers were predictable and sometimes even more ignorant than expected. He said he still believes that Iraq had posed an imminent threat to U.S. security and even mentioned Hussein's threat to kill Bush senior as if it were, by itself, a sensible reason to take two nations into war. Predictably, he mentioned the war on terrorism and the need to take the fight to 'them' rather than wait for terrorists to come to us. (All of this has been repeatedly dismissed by terrorism experts who note that the war in Iraq is creating more terrorists every day we occupy the nation.) And he told us that he couldn't say for sure whether or not he'd withdraw support from the war if the surge in troops didn't work because, "I am not a military or foreign policy expert."

Sickeningly, when I asked Weldon about Martin Luther King's assertion that a nation that spends more money on military expenses than on programs of social uplift is approaching spiritual decline, adding that our nation spends more than 400 billion on defense each year, Weldon replied, "If I had it my way I would shut down the Federal Dept. of Education and give money to states." Adding, "Defense spending is not enough."

On the same day we met with Weldon, active duty U.S. Army Officer Lt. Col. Paul Yingling said that there is little hope for victory in Iraq, and former CIA director George Tenet asserted that the Bush administration rushed to war without a serious debate about the threat posed by Saddam. Tenet also said Bush misused his "slam-dunk" statement in the rush to war. These facts are lost upon Weldon, a blind, ardent Bush supporter.

Weldon told us that the war has been won. It's only the battle for peace we need to win. And the most he could say about Tenet's point was, "I'll read the book."

So you might ask - what did we accomplish? A lot, actually. Needless to say, we didn't change Weldon's mind. There's no changing the mind of a man who entreats ideology over the facts. Our meeting with Dave Weldon was the culmination of years of dedicated activism on the part of everyday Brevard citizens clamoring for peace, a broader effort that began when a few dozen of us met at the now defunct Greenhouse café in downtown Melbourne. Those were the days when undercover officers from the Sheriff's Office were spying on our activities; when we organized two pre-war rallies that would lead to 400-500 people marching through downtown Melbourne in opposition to the war. Four years later, the Brevard county peace movement is pervasive and expanding rapidly.

Perhaps our footsteps and our chants for an end to the bloodshed are getting so loud that even war supporters like Weldon can't ignore us anymore. Perhaps he knows it's because of the peace movement than an under-funded, blatantly anti-war candidate, Dr. Bowman, gave Weldon his most serious congressional race in a decade last November.

In any case, the greatest value of our meeting lies in the message it sends to everyone reading this - your voice can be heard over the din of politicians, if you take up the banner and live the life of a true citizen. That five everyday peace activists got to take their grievances and opinions to the person in power is a reminder that, at the end of the day, we are the ones who sign the checks of elected officials. And we can sign pink slips and end wars anytime we muster up enough political and moral will-power. That time is now.

*Author's note: In January 2008, anti-choice, Religious Right Republican, David Weldon, announced he would not run for reelection in the November 2008 election. Weldon rose to power in 1994, served seven terms, and was an ardent backer of George W. Bush.

—Originally published at TowardFreedom.com on June 19, 2007.

INTERVIEW WITH RENOWNED PEACE MUSICIAN, JESSE COLIN YOUNG

>K

Renowned singer-songwriter Jesse Colin Young is best known for the peace anthem "Get Together" first released in 1967 with the Youngbloods. On October 4th 2005, Young celebrated his prolific career by releasing a double-CD *The Very Best of Jesse Colin Young,* which spans his more than 30-year songwriting career. His first ever "Best Of" release, the package features a torrent of classics including "Song for Juli," "Darkness Darkness," "The Peace Song," and "Get Together." The CD set also includes three new songs, "Sweet Good Times," "Lovin' You," and "Eyes On the Prize," as well as "Imagine/What's Going On," a tune that melds John Lennon's "Imagine" and Marvin Gaye's "What's Going On" into one.

In 2006, I talked to Young about the influence of the ideal of peace on his work.

JN: *So much of your music concentrates on the theme of peace. Are you involved with the peace movement at this time? Or are your thoughts on what we're doing in Iraq a little more complicated?*

JCY: [laughing] No I don't think it's more complicated. I'd love to see the troops home....I don't think we ever should have invaded. The way I'm active in the peace movement is by playing my music, and by writing songs about it. That's one of the reasons I still play is because "Get Together" is still a touchstone, and other songs too in my catalogue, really a touchstone for that yearning after peace which everyone who has ever held a baby in their arms or maybe even had a blissfully restful weekend off somewhere by a stream knows of. Children bring it on stronger I think, and you want them to be safe and you want to be safe to bring them up, so it's a deep.

JN: *In September 2005 nearly 300 people gathered to protest the war in Melbourne, Florida where you're going to be performing.*

JCY: I was thrilled, a month ago we were in Monclear, New Jersey — want to talk about upper-middle class and beyond, upscale bedroom community to New York City. My road manager and best friend Vito was on his way to the sound check and he said, "Jess there were demonstrators... in Montclair." And then next day I see the paper... and there's two very middle-class, middle-aged looking people on the front page and one has a t-shirt that says "peace activist"... and the other guy who was a scientist or something had a "worst president ever" t-shirt ever, and I thought this is wonderful... These were not the kind of people that I would expect to be on their front porch being photographed and opening themselves to the grief that can come with that.... I'm thrilled to see this, I've been praying for it and wondering when it would happen. And wondering how there could be so many, what I would call cowards, in the Congress to give this war to the president in the first place. I guess it was just because we were all so scared and somehow they were able to put their agenda, well they lied to us. And we thought, oh well maybe this will make us safer. Umm, or, that's the only excuse I can think of.

JN: *[laughing] You're trying real hard there.*

JCY: I imagine it was trying to save their political careers. And it made me hearken back to the time when in the beginning of the country when we served only for service and only for four years. And then we went back to being farmers....When you make service a life-long career you have to make a lot more compromises. That's the nicest way I can put it. And even the finest men and women get compromised beyond where they can really stand up on an issue like that and say, we have no real proof of weapons of mass destruction, I'm sorry you can't send my sons and daughters over there, forget it.... So I'm glad people are pissed off.

JN: *When did you write 'Peace Song'?*

JCY: It was written during Vietnam. I started playing it in the Youngbloods, I think in 1969, and recorded it on my first solo album which was made while the Youngbloods were coming to an end in 70, or 71. It's from an album called *Together*. That was the only sense I could make out of the Vietnam war after agonizing for four or five years: every time we kill someone we make ten enemies or twenty; everyone in their family hates us. That's the only thing I could think of, the simplest thing: we can't kill our way to peace, there's just no way.

JN: *How do you feel about being by and large being identified with your song, "Get Together"?*

JCY: I just got real lucky. That song is not it's just not about me and my career. It's just pure chance that I connected with a song that I did not write. The first time I heard it I just fell in love with it, and I ran back stage and I asked the guy – I had heard it at an open mic in the Village – and I said, "you've got to teach me that song." And I have never done that before or since. So I fell in love with it and I took it into rehearsal the next day with the Youngbloods.

Every time I sing it's like church. This past summer I sang it at the Triple A radio convention in a room with maybe 75 or 100 people. No PA, nothing. Just acoustic. And people cry. They're crying because we are where we are or because it touches something in them very strongly. These are tough professionals in the music business weeping because that song touches the core of that and reminds us how far we are from it. What can I say, it's such a jewel and it's on the air everyday and it's doing its work for peace. When I'm down here folding my kids laundry, "Get Together" is doing its work. What a privilege for me to be involved in that or to be able to sing it with people at every show. It was always my favorite part of church, singing, and still is. It touches that universal longing, whether your Buddhist or a Christian or whatever, it's all there in the teachings.... .

After singing "Get Together lets try to love one another," that was the well, yeah, ok, what do we do? What's the next step? That song ("Peace Song"), I found myself weeping and agonizing over the war and just trying to figure out what it is we could possibly do.

There are some songs that we'll be recording this next year that are coming at it from another angle, a song called 'Walk the Talk About Love.' It's time we do something. To carry the dream of loving each other is wonderful, to put it to use and get out there and walk it in whatever we do in the world. And perhaps in demonstrations, too. It's kind of a call for action.

Jn: *Can you share a few lines from "Walk the Talk About Love"?*

Jcy: "Are you tired of the struggle for money and fame/ you let vanity rule you it will drive you insane (I know that from perfect experience)/ right here in the garden we have chosen to live/ it's not what you can get my brother, my sister, it's about what you can give. And the chorus is "We're talking about love. Love, lets talk about love. Must be time we learn to walk our talk about love."

Jn: *You have a musical career seriously dedicated to the theme of peace. Is that an expression of your nature or is it something you fell into, did you gravitate toward peace?*

Jcy: No, it's not in my nature. I remember my manager, when I started singing, he said, I really like the angry young man side of you a lot better. Why are you singing this song? I said, I think this song is my future. And it has always been like a mantra. And every time I sing it, I remind myself, yes, this is what I am struggling for: peace in my heart, peace in my home, peace and justice in my community, peace in my nation, peace in the world. But it really starts in your heart.

For more info on Young go to http://www.jessecolinyoung.com

THE OTHER ELECTION STORY: THE DEMISE OF A THIRD PARTY PRESENCE IN THE U.S.

⌖

The election results are in. For better or worse, George Bush has been reelected. And while progressives as well as moderates in both the Democratic and Republican parties ponder the daunting possibilities of four more years of W (i.e. the wars on peace, women, separation of church and state, fiscal responsibility and civil liberties), the president having been reelected is only half of the story.

Despite Ralph Nader's warning to Democrats on November 3rd to "stay tuned: We are just beginning to fight" ("Nader Ends Presidential Campaign," Associated Press, November 3, 2004) the 2004 election has solidified a 12 year decline in third party voting. Whereas more than 20 million votes were cast for third party candidates in 1992, 10 million in 1996, and nearly 4 million in 2000, just over 1 million votes (less than 1 percent) were cast for candidates outside of the two major parties in 2004. Not since 1984, the last time third party candidates received less than 1 percent of the vote, has the hegemony of the two major parties been so apparent.

While some may attribute this year's decline to the Democrats' successful legal campaign to keep Nader's name off of the ballot in many states, much of the opposition to third party candidacies came

127

from within their own ranks. Speaking on behalf of liberals everywhere, fearful of the prospect of Bush's reelection, *The Nation's* editorial board implored Nader not to run; even an editorial in *IMPACT* featured a plea for voters *not* to vote for Nader. But such invectives were as much an assault on the plurality voting method employed to elect the president as they were attacks on candidates such as Nader.

The plurality voting method, which is the most commonly applied method in the U.S., requires voters to choose only one candidate, ruling out the option of selecting a secondary choice. And because the plurality method does not allow third party voters to specify a second or third choice, a vote for Nader, for instance, may effectively result in a vote for Bush. In fact, many analysts believe that the 2000 election would not have come down to a few thousand potentially miscounted ballots in Florida, had the preference of third party voters been taken into consideration in determining whether Bush or Gore should become president. In a November 6 *New York Times* article, Sandy Maisel of the Goldfarb Center for Public Policy at Colby College was quoted as saying, "Those who chose Nader over Al Gore in 2000 realized what they'd done and bolted for Kerry" ("Nader Is Left With Fewer Votes, and Friends, After '04 Race," *New York Times* online, November 6, 2004).

According to Anthony Lorenzo, chair of the Political Action Committee Coalition for Instant Runoff Voting (CIRV) in Florida, without revamping the voting methodology minor parties can only go so far. "Minor parties–the Progressive Party, specifically, as it was the most successful historically, I think–have a destiny, according to historical data, to get so far in our system," says Lorenzo. "Once they begin to win, they are merged with one of the majors by the major party adopting some or all of their platform–Social Security, etc. Other than that, they are destined to fade away in a plurality system and be a nuisance to the majors."

Rob Richie, executive director for the CVD, believes IRV will achieve fair representation in the White House. "We've put our money on IRV for a couple of reasons. One, there's a simple logic to it, which is people have preferences as long as their first choice has a chance to win. Typically, they want that person to win," says Richie. At the same time, he says, if a person's first choice fails to climb into the top two candidates, his or her second choice should be counted.

Robert Loring, owner and director of AccurateDemocracy.com, also believes IRV is an effective voting method. "The election of a president, governor, or mayor who can veto legislation needs to be linked to the rules and time of election for the legislature," he said. "Otherwise the two powers are more likely to reach a deadlock over differences in policy and funding. IRV then is the best rule for electing a chief executive."

According to Lorenzo, whose group CIRV is working to bring IRV to communities throughout Florida, minority parties aren't the only ones with something to gain from IRV but so do the two dominant parties. "There are many examples of how IRV would help this or that group," Lorenzo says. "For instance, in 2000, Al Gore would have won Florida according to results, assuming Greens would have voted for Gore second. In 1992, Ross Perot took enough votes from the Republicans to elect Clinton and defeat Bush. The pendulum swings both ways. The point of IRV is to ensure that the winner is supported by the majority of Americans. IRV on its own doesn't change anything other than the way the votes are tabulated." Notable supporters of IRV include Democrat Howard Dean, and even Republican Senator John McCain.

Lorenzo says IRV benefits everyone involved, especially voters. "Everyone benefits because we get a government that is truly representative of the majority who vote. By requiring a majority with IRV, we ensure that most people are happy with the winners of elections. Also, in areas where second runoff elections are conducted, these second elections are expensive and elimination of second elections saves taxpayers money," Lorenzo explains. "In my city, Sarasota [Florida], that amounts to $37,000 per election. They are conducted every 2 years and there has been a runoff each year since they reinstated runoffs. San Francisco has demonstrated that IRV also has another interesting side effect: cooperation amongst competitors for the same office and an election almost devoid of negative campaigning. When candidates are inspired to talk issues, we all benefit from the ability to make a more informed decision as voters. I think everyone is sick of the draft dodger, traitor, etc. attacks characteristic of the more visible races. They turn everyone off and it is a convenient way to avoid discussing issues."

But after years of witnessing their vote inadvertently support the candidate most antipathetic to their real choice, third party voters are now caving to the realistic demands of the current voting system: vote Democrat or Republican, or don't bother voting. "Without IRV," explains Lorenzo, "people fear voting their conscience. I mean, look at Dennis Kucinich's race for the Democratic nomination and how he faired. He got very few votes as most Democrats were trying to pick the candidate who could beat Bush. In fact, everyone I spoke to supported Kucinich, yet they feared he could not win. In IRV, we can support the best candidate. We can vote our conscience."

A change in voting methodology would likely increase voter turnout, reduce costs in some places, and, at the least, contribute to the expansion of an often stifled, calcified exchange of ideas. Despite the decline in presidential election minority-party voting, history has shown that millions of Americans do prefer a plethora of candidates to choose from. But to stay the current course, the U.S. runs the risk of not only losing important dissenting voices from minority party politicians, but also risks the alienation of millions of Americans who want more than to cynically cast votes for the less despised candidate.

Though the nation is understandably concerned with the victor and loser of the 2004 election, the ever-increasing tendency of voters to sacrifice their true vision of America in exchange for a murky reflection of that ideal is equally as significant and deserves the attention of the country.

—Originally published in the December-January
2005 issue of IMPACT press.

SUPERDELEGATES AND THE
ILLUSION OF DEMOCRACY

>-K

The 2008 Democratic Party presidential nomination race has given many people an education on the behind-the-scenes business of electing a president and the role played by superdelegates. We now know (if we didn't already) that a small group of 796 officials and party leaders control about 20 percent of the power to choose the Democratic candidate. The millions of Democratic Party members weathering the snow, rain, and after-work races to the polls "control" the remaining 80 percent.

Speaking on "The Diane Rehm Show," political consultant Tad Devine maintained that superdelegates weren't meant to infringe on the Democratic process of choosing a presidential candidate, they're meant to offer a peer review aspect to the democratic process ("The Democratic Convention," February 11, 2008).

In an op-ed piece for the New York Times, Devine writes that Democrats created superdelegates after the 1980 election so that party leaders would be better represented at the convention ("Superdelegates, Back Off," February 10, 2008): "Many party leaders felt that the delegates would actually be more representative of all Democratic voters if we had more elected officials on the convention floor to offset the more liberal impulses of party activists." If party leaders really wanted to have the voters' voices represented, they would simply use their votes to decide on a presidential nominee. Party leaders are apparently so fearful of entrusting even the small group of delegates who attend the convention on behalf of millions of voters that "superdelegates" are needed to guard the White House. What about the more liberal impulses of every-day party members? And why do we need to offset the work of "party activists" as if "activism" is something which the party wishes to discourage? If anything, more voters should be encouraged to engage in activism within the party. And how exactly does Devine define "more liberal impulses"? He doesn't say. Perhaps he means true universal healthcare, drastically reducing the Federal military budget, drastically increasing the minimum wage, or giving the airwaves back to the public.

Superdelegates were also created, writes Devine, to "provide unity at the nominating convention." He urges superdelegates to refrain from pledging their support for either Clinton or Obama before, as he writes, "the voters have had their say." While it's nice of Devine to urge superdelegates to refrain from picking the Democrat's presidential nominee before the people have the chance to vote, he falls short of urging the party to make changes that bar superdelegates from pledging support. One must ask, "If the voters get it 'wrong,' will Devine and other so-called voices of reason urge party bosses to lead the ignorant masses to the correct trough?" His answer: "After listening to the voters, the superdelegates can do what the Democratic Party's rules originally envisioned. They can ratify the results of the primaries and caucuses in all 50 states by moving as a bloc toward the candidate who has proved to be the strongest in the contest that matters...."

Democratic strategist and superdelegate Donna Brazile said that superdelegates make up only 20% of the vote and that they're representative of everyday Americans (The Diane Rehm Show, February, 11, 2008). But that's just it! If the average superdelegate is so much like the average voter, why not allow all parties an equal share of the vote, no less or more? Moreover, how can one downplay the fact that a small group of less than one-thousand party insiders carry 1/5 of the weight of nominating our party's candidate?

According to one estimate, superdelegates comprise just 0.000007 percent of the voting population, but about 20 percent of the power to choose the Democratic nominee. Consider that the nearly 4 million voters in California are represented by 350 delegates; more than 400,000 voters in South Carolina have their choice represented by only 37 delegates; and Georgia's one-million Democratic primary voters are represented by just 71 delegates. In total, five and a half million voters are represented by less than 500 delegates. That's about 11,000 voters per delegate. Whom do superdelegates represent? Themselves.

This is what Hillary Clinton was counting on. According to *ABC News*, Hillary wined and dined 17 uncommitted superdelegates. At a press conference Hillary defended her focus on superdelegates despite trailing in the delegate race. "Superdelgeates, so called, are in the process because many of them are long time officials, long time party activists who can exercise independent judgment about who is best able to both present the Democratic party case and win the White House," said Clinton. Asked by a reporter whether or not such reasoning would convince voters Clinton said: "I think that we are following what was determined to be an appropriate process for picking the nominees" ("Superdelegate Showdown: Clinton switches focus from Pennsylvania voters to persuading crucial delegates," March 14, 2008). Simply put, Hillary Clinton doesn't mind wining the nomination without the support of the people whom she would represent. Her new focus is on schmoozing party elite rather than convincing the populous, the backbone of the Democratic Party. She, too, seems to agree that American citizens need an overseer to choose the proper representative.

The utilization of superdelegates is tantamount to ensuring that if the game doesn't go the way party insiders want it to, there's a mechanism to ensure they can have the final say. Either the Democratic Party believes in democracy, which requires a trust in the party base, or it does not. It should not, however, give .000007% of party members more than 20% of the decision making. The use of super-delegates amounts to a hierarchal control of the party dressed in the visage of democracy.

How can Democrats take on the gulf between haves and have nots if the disparity between rich and poor is so obscenely manifested in the very process by which we elect our representatives? It's time for many Americans to realize that the democracy they've believed in is a fairy tale. More importantly, Americans need to stop asking and start forcing their way into the insider enclaves that have so *generously* taken over the burden of governing our future.

Versions of this piece originally appeared at TowardFreedom.com on February 19, 2008 and the March 2008 issue of Z magazine.

Perpetual REVOLT

HEADING OFF
THE CULTURE WAR:
SHARED VALUES OF
RELIGIOUS, SPIRITUAL &
SECULAR PROGRESSIVES

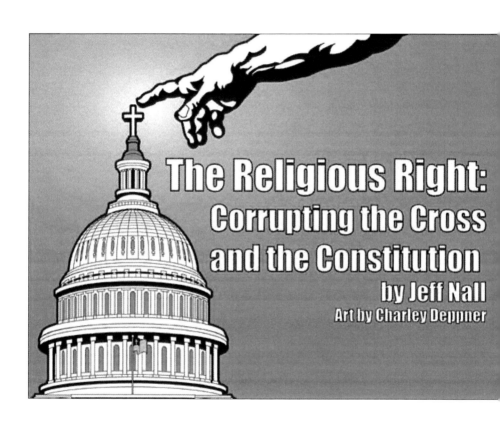

The Religious Right:
Corrupting the Cross
and the Constitution
by Jeff Nall
Art by Charley Deppner

THE RELIGIOUS RIGHT: CORRUPTING
THE CROSS AND THE CONSTITUTION

>K

Although physical in their material composition both the Christian crucifix and the American Constitution have transcended their material significance. Both are objects that have become sacred, evoking reverence and great emotion in their representation of some great ideal. Both have affected their followers with such passion, myriads of men and women have given their lives in pursuit of their grand and noble ideals. Each symbols of great power, both were a part of an astonishingly expedient rise to power (Christianity in just a few centuries, and the U.S. in less than two). The differences between these objects, of course, are far greater than they are similar. In one, we find a profound religious expression of faith, an intimate belief beyond the temporal world, while the other speaks to a purely earthly purpose. One symbolizes the Christian faith and the dedication of that faith's holy author, God. The other, the Constitution, was the work of earthly architects like Benjamin Franklin and James Madison, and purely concerns itself with the governance of our nation, here and now. Though reasonable minds prevailed at the ratification of the Constitution, the call to unite these vastly incongruent artifacts has never been more clamorous than it is today.

Recently, the fight to keep God and government separated was

137

waged by a resilient minority in Brevard County, Florida. When two parents from different households–one a Buddhist, the other an atheist–teamed up to stop to their children's high school from holding public graduation ceremonies at a local mega-church, Calvary Chapel, which refused to secularize the venue by covering or taking down its 15-20 foot cross and other iconography, the notably conservative community collectively gasped.

Parent Sonia Marquez told the local paper, *Florida Today*, in a May 17, 2005 article, "The place is spacious, and it has nothing to do with religion. It's being rented." In the same article, another parent, Richard Warner, said, "A lot of parents at Bayside [High School] are just furious at what these people are trying to pull." Suzanne Beers, also a parent, told the newspaper in a May 15, 2005 article, "It's taking away from the kids to make it a religious, political, governmental battle." One surly local, angry over the attempt to move the graduation, told one of the parents, via email, "Certainly you can dedicate your cause to something worthwhile but no, you feel you can impose your will on the majority who want the graduation at Calvary."

With the assistance of Americans United for the Separation of Church and State, the parents took the Brevard County School Board to court just a few days before the first of four graduations were set to begin. Federal District Judge Gregory A. Presnell determined that there wasn't enough time to stop the graduations from taking place. Judge Presnell did, however, side with the plaintiffs in agreeing that the school board had violated 12th grade student Jennifer Musgrove's rights by wrongly choosing a religious venue for the event. According to a May 19 *Florida Today* story, in court Presnell said, "It's clear to me a secular facility without those icons should have been chosen in order to protect the interests of everyone..."

By October 25, 2005, the Brevard County School Board decided to save the estimated $100,000 it would have inevitably lost in a no-win court battle and gave in to demands that prevent graduations from being held in "houses of worship in which religious iconography is visible to participants or to anyone in attendance on either the outside or the inside of the building." Before the final settlement, the legal tussle immediately became top news throughout Central Florida. Opinion polls conducted by the local newspaper and local TV stations showed overwhelming support for not changing the location of the graduation, with fewer than 20 percent objecting to the use of a church. Christians angry over the audacity of the plaintiffs, who included published atheist author Dianna Narciso, sent vitriolic e-mails, drove by the plaintiffs' homes, and, in general, complained of their disregard for the wishes of the apparent majority who were fine with the venue.

The rift created by this local battle over where to hold graduation ceremonies reveals one of the toxic elements responsible for destroying the edifice of the wall between church and state today: Many Christians believe the wall is an atheist's war on Christianity and belief. The fact that those willing to take tough stands on issues like school prayer, the Pledge of Allegiance, and graduation ceremonies are often atheists and non-traditional believers doesn't help to discount such a perception either. But, as is the case with this issue, the truth is often deeper than surface perceptions.

After contacting numerous area religious leaders, I discovered that many of them were also opposed to holding the graduations at the church. A local Jewish leader, Cantor Pat Hickman of Temple Israel in Viera, Florida, said she agreed that graduations should not be held at churches. "I think most of the people in my community were uncomfortable with the idea of having a public school graduation in a facility that had very strong symbols of one particular faith. I think that there are lots of other places that public schools can have their ceremonies, where they don't exclude anybody or make anybody feel uncomfortable even if there are just a few people in the graduating class who are another faith. It didn't seem appropriate to me," Hickman said.

Swamiji Chid Ghan Anand, spiritual leader of the Shri Shiv Dham Hindu Temple in Orlando, outside of Brevard, concurred. "[The venue] should not be related to a religion," he said, "because there are many people going to that school who are not Christian or maybe not related to Christians or maybe don't want to be related to Christians."

But support for the separation of church and state wasn't limited to Hindus, atheists, and Jews. Representing a large number of Christians who support church-state separation, the Rev. Alicia S. Rapp of the Florida-based Palm Bay Riviera United Church of Christ, explained that just a few days after the contended graduations began taking place at a church, she was frustrated to find the boundaries of separation of church and state garishly blurred before her very eyes. Not only was her son's sixth grade public school graduation held at a Presbyterian church, but after the ceremony, members of the church enticed children with free Tootsie-Roll pops and proceeded to give them flyers regarding the church's basketball camp and its vacation Bible school. When Rapp reached her car, she found yet another piece of church literature on her windshield: "And I know that the church was just thinking, 'Hey this is a great time to market our church.' But I think of it as crossing the line."

Rapp went on to explain that her church goes out of its way to ensure it doesn't cross the important boundary between God and government. "We don't allow politics to cross over into our congregation... When I preach from the pulpit I also preach about the war and those kinds of things... but I don't say if you vote for George Bush or one way or another. And that's the separation of church and state issue."

Unfortunately, clearer Christian voices of reason like Rapp's are often overwhelmed by wealthy conservative Christian organizations that flood the TV and radio airwaves with the theme of persecution. Essentially, they believe that atheists or secularists are conspiring, with the separation of church and state as its filet knife, to carve religion from the bone of American society. In fact, persecution propaganda has so infected the consciousness of the American people that an October 2005 poll conducted by the Anti-Defamation League shows 64 percent of the nation feels religion is "under attack."

How does such an absurd, conspiratorial idea become recognized by the populace as a conventional truism? The answer: James Dobson, one of the Religious Right's most powerful zealots. Dobson is the founder of Focus on the Family, a Christian outreach organization that produces 10 monthly magazines, makes about $136 million annually and communicates with 200 million listeners through its daily radio program. In 1996, Dobson explained in a lengthy letter titled "Was America a Christian Nation?" that "secularists" have undertaken an "unprecedented campaign to secularize our society and 'de-moralize' our institutions from the top down," and are now moving on to "complete the task of immobilizing and silencing conservative Christians."

According to the religious Web site ReTakingAmerica.com, during the 2003 protest of plans to remove the Ten Commandments monument at Alabama's state judicial building, Dobson told protestors he believed—starting with the court's 1962 decision to "remov[e] prayer from the schools"—that "the Supreme Court has been on a campaign to eliminate that perspective from public life." In his aforementioned letter, Dobson said the secularists plot is in part "to convince the American people that Christians, specifically those with conservative inclinations, are in violation of the Constitution whenever they advocate their views beyond the front doors of their sanctuaries." He continued, "Liberal activists would have us believe our founding fathers were terrified at the prospect of Christians participating in the political process. This led them, we're told, to protect the government from religious meddling. But no such provision appears in the Constitution or any of the foundational documents."

Dobson went on to write in the letter that the purpose of the separation of church and state, which he notes "is found only in one of Jefferson's letters," and tends to dismiss as an improper reading of the Establishment Clause, was intended to be a one-way street deal–to protect "religion from governmental interference." Dobson is frequently quoted as having said that the separation of church and state isn't substantiated by the Constitution and therefore an invention of secularists seeking to destroy Christianity. In an interview with Larry King on his September 5, 2003 show, Dobson explained his position thusly: "[The Establishment Clause] says Congress shall make no law establishing a religion or interfering with the free exercise thereof. That's the clause that all of this has come from. There is nothing in there about separation of church and state."

While the Religious Right clamors over God-less liberals and "secularist" plots, the reality is that a June 2005 Associate Press/ Ipsos "Religious Attitudes" poll showed that fewer than three percent of Americans "don't believe in God." In fact, America continues to be one of the most religious countries among industrialized nations. According to the poll, which surveyed the various religious perspectives of 10 nations, the U.S. is second only to Mexico in pious inclinations, with 70 percent of Americans professing they "know God really exists" and "have no doubts about it."

The true impetus behind the Religious Right's scramble to mesh its ultra-conservative Christian theology with politics is likely to have far more to do with the fact the U.S. is becoming increasingly pluralistic as the overall population is less dominated by Protestantism. For instance, in July 2004, the National Opinion Research Center 2004 report, "The Vanishing Protestant Majority," showed that the percentage of the nation's Protestants had dropped from 60.4 percent in 1988 to 52.4 percent in 2002.

Undoubtedly aware of the rise of religions such as Islam, Hinduism, Wicca, Taoism, Native American religion, Buddhism, Sikhism, and many others, which have doubled and tripled their members between 1991 and 2001, the Religious Right is likely far less concerned with atheism than it is with the end of Christianity's spiritual hegemony in the United States–particularly their brand of extremist belief. Nevertheless, the constitutional revisionism and incessant rhetoric of fundamentalists have led many Christians to misconstrue fervent efforts to uphold the Constitution's unbiased protection of the freedom of religion for all as aversion for Christianity. Nothing could be further from the case.

Christianity is not at all the monolith that well-funded ideologues like Dobson and Falwell would have you believe. With more

than 30 different groups residing under its banner of Christianity including Catholic, Baptist, nondenominational, Quaker, Lutherans, Church of God, Pentecostal, and Presbyterian, Christianity has been and continues to be aided by the First Amendment's guarantee of the separation of church and state as much if not more than any other group in the United States. Those inclined to mock such an assertion fail to realize the lurking danger Christians face as religious leaders vie for increased political power and seek to transform the U.S. into a so-called "Christian nation."

Consider the results of one of a 2003 poll conducted and reported by the Barna Research Group (BRG), an evangelical Christian research group. It stated that fewer than 10 percent of born-again Christians truly possess a biblical worldview, which BRG defined as accepting Biblically-derived absolute moral truths, and accepting these six core beliefs: "The accuracy of biblical teaching, the sinless nature of Jesus, the literal existence of Satan, the omnipotence and omniscience of God, salvation by grace alone, and the personal responsibility to evangelize." The poll showed, according to BRG, that other Christians groups were even more out of touch, with only seven percent of Protestants, two percent of "adults who attend mainline Protestant churches," and less than one percent of Catholics conforming to a 'true' biblical worldview.

In January 2004, the group audaciously reported that only 51 percent of U.S. Protestant pastors have what it deemed a true biblical worldview. While the poll proves that a plethora of diversity exists under the housing of what we call the Christian religion, organizations such as BRG, which is an arm of the evangelical Barna Group, have no trouble grading believers according to its own vision of what proper belief should be. As James Madison put it in 1785: "Who does not see the same authority which can establish Christianity, in exclusion of all other Religions, may establish with the same ease any particular sect of Christians, in exclusion of all other Sects." The point is that the separation of church and state protects the freedom of Christians to practice their religion according to the dictates of their own conscience, their own interpretation of scripture.

The idea that separating church and state benefits the Christian religion is not a new one. In fact, one of the seminal proponents of the separation was a Christian who anticipated the founding fathers. Setting out with the specific purpose of severing religion from the workings of civil government (and vice-versa), the renowned Protestant philosopher, John Locke, in 1689, wrote "A Letter Concerning Toleration." Far from trying to perpetuate an atheistic apocalypse by vanquishing religion from society, Locke sought to overthrow the spiritual tyranny of those politicizing the realm of God and true religion. Having lived during an age when "fiery zealots" wielded the power to "persecute, torment, destroy, and kill other men upon pretence of religion," Locke argued for an end to the religious strife which harmed Christians as much as it did Jews and nonbelievers: "And upon this ground I affirm that the magistrate's power extends not to the establishing of any article of faith, or forms of worship, by the force of his laws." Locke's take on this issue is of particular importance because he is not only one of the first people to put the separation of church and state into a doctrine, but he also profoundly influenced the American founders.

According to Locke, civil society is solely concerned with the civil interests of its members, such as the procurement and preservation of physical health and property, all of which are exclusively bound to the physical world. "The business of true religion," however, explained Locke, is to regulate "men's lives according to the rules of virtue and piety," not to obtain "ecclesiastical dominion, nor to the exercising of compulsive force." Locke believed those, such as Pat Robertson, who try to convolute the very different businesses of government and religion, seek to prostitute religion in order to gain political power. And no church or religious organization, no matter how powerful or truly representative of God, has a right to issue legal dictates to or through the civil authorities. "[T]he power of civil government," Locke wrote, "is confined to the care of the things of this world, and hath nothing to do with the world to come."

While today, fundamentalists frequently demonize the principle of separation of church and state as a heathen ploy to eradicate religion, the truth is that definite believers like Locke were among the first thinkers to highlight the absurdity and pure fallacy of combining religion and government. Ironically, it was the philosopher Thomas Hobbes, widely believed to be an atheist, who wrote in 1651 that religion should have a significant role in the state, primarily as a tool of the state. Locke, on the other hand, not only advocated the separation of church and state, believing it would benefit both the state and the church, he also thought it would preserve the integrity and freedom of religion. "...I ask, what power can be given to the magistrate for the suppression of an idolatrous church, which may not, in time and place, be made use of to the ruin of an orthodox one?"

Seventeenth-century Christian Roger Williams was another noted advocate for ending the entanglement of religion and government. In 1644, more than 150 years before the deist Thomas Jefferson spoke of the "wall of separation between church and state," Williams, an English clergyman, expressed his concern over opening "a gap in the hedge, or wall of separation between the garden of the church and the wilderness of the world." In his 2005 article in *Church and State*, Edwin S. Gaustad, professor of history and religious studies emeritus at the University of California, Riverside, writes that Williams "advocated the scariest political heresy of his day: namely, that a civil institution could survive without the supporting arm of the church."

Later, in the mid 1800s, French historian Alexis de Tocqueville, a Roman Catholic reporting on the rise of American democracy, wrote that he was initially shocked to learn that the "spirit of religion and the spirit of freedom" in America were not "pursuing courses diametrically opposed to each other." Upon coming into contact with "several" priests, he found "that they mainly attributed the peaceful dominion of religion in their country to the separation of Church and State. I do not hesitate to affirm that during my stay in America I did not meet with a single individual, of the clergy or of the laity, who was not of the same opinion upon this point."

Conservative Christians bemoan the Supreme Court's decision ruling school prayer unconstitutional, but it is interesting to note that one of the most important Christian supporters of church-state separation emphatically agreed with the ruling. Directly contradicting James Dobson's view of the decision, Martin Luther King, in 1965, told *Playboy* magazine that he agreed with the U.S. Supreme Court's decision ruling school mandated prayer unconstitutional. He said: "I endorse it. I think it was correct. Contrary to what many have said, it sought to outlaw neither prayer nor belief in God. In a pluralistic society such as ours, who is to determine what prayer shall be spoken, and by whom? Legally, constitutionally, or otherwise, the state certainly has no such right. I am strongly opposed to the efforts that have been made to nullify the decision."

It is also worth noting the powerful argument articulated by Justice Hugo Black in the 1962 decision, which King endorsed.

> It is an unfortunate fact of history that when some of the very groups which had most strenuously opposed the established Church of England found themselves sufficiently in control of colonial governments in this country to write their own prayers into law, they passed laws making their own religion the official religion of their respective colonies. ...[A]s late as the time of the Revolutionary War, there were established churches in at least 8 of the 13 former colonies and established religions in at least 4 of the other 5.
>
> ...By the time of the adoption of the Constitution, our history shows that there was a widespread awareness among many Americans of the dangers of a union of Church and State. ...The Constitution was intended to avert a part of this danger by leaving the government of this country in the hands of the people rather than in the hands of the monarch.

King seemed to echo this sentiment when he stated that the church "is not the master or the servant of the state, but rather the conscience of the state. It must be the guide and the critic of the state, and never its tool."

American history is also filled with Christian presidents who expressly defended the separation of church and state. Among the more devout Christians and former presidents, Jimmy Carter has been vocal on the church-state matter. On December 5, he told *The Daily Show*'s Jon Stewart that he is greatly concerned about "the merger of ... religion and politics. Because I happen to be a Christian and I think my religion teaches me that you should render unto Caesar the things that are Caesar's and unto God the things that are God's." He went on to complain that "there has been an increasing merger in this country of fundamentalism on the religious side, fundamentalism on the political side, and the two have come together."

Despite the fact that many important Christian minds have long upheld and encouraged the separation of church and state, the Religious Right has successfully planted in the minds of many Americans that one can't be both a supporter of the separation of church and state and a Christian. Take for instance the response Brevard County Lutheran Michele Paccione received when she contacted her county commissioners, complaining that she felt they had infringed on the constitutional separation of church and state when they endorsed a religious, Christ-centered youth program, which had also been promoted by the county's schools. Brevard County Commissioner Helen Voltz responded via email, writing: "What an oxymoron!!!! A Christian who believes in the separation of church & state? What??? What is your definition of a Christian? The Bible says a Christian is 'Christlike.' Do you think for one minute that Jesus would support the separation of church & state?"

While Voltz's opinion is shared by a growing number of Christians, it's simply absurd to believe that Christianity and the First Amendment don't go hand in hand. According to Rob Boston, assistant director of communications for Americans United for the Separation of Church and State, Christians have always played an invaluable role in defending the wall. "Many religious people support and defend the separation of church and state—and those folks add a powerful and needed voice to this issue. For example, in Washington, the Baptist Joint Committee for Religious Liberty strongly supports church-state separation, arguing that the wall of separation is the best vehicle to defend freedom of conscience for all. Over the years, Americans United has worked with Methodists, Lutherans...Presbyterians, Unitarians, Quakers, Seventh day Adventists and many others."

The latest group of Christians standing in defense of church-state separation is the newly formed Christian Alliance for Progress (CAP), which is based out of Jacksonville, Florida. Specifically purposed to save the integrity of the Christian faith and combat the extremist agenda of the Religious Right, CAP and its growing number of supporters "reaffirm a well-established American commitment to a clear separation of church and state," believing that the separation "helps ensure liberty and justice for all Americans–not just those who are like-minded."

Rev. Timothy Simpson, CAP's director of religious affairs, says his organization, which Jerry Falwell has denounced as "hardly 'Christian,'" fears the consequences of the government's growing relationship with religion. "...We don't need the government to be subsidizing us," he said, "to be giving us sweet-heart deals, special favors. That's inappropriate. Those kinds of things are what caused so many problems in other parts of the world where Christians who ruled did so unjustly, and used the name of Jesus Christ in a tyrannical fashion."

One of the best reasons for Christians to stand beside nonbelievers and religious minorities in defense of church-state separation is precisely because it protects the religion from a wholesale takeover by the radical Religious Right and the absolute molestation of Christ's message of love, justice, and brotherhood. Consider the men behind what we call the Religious Right; consider their words. After the 9/11, Jerry Falwell appeared on *The 700 Club*, telling viewers "the pagans and the abortionists and the feminists and the gays and the lesbians who are actively trying to make an alternative lifestyle, the ACLU, People for the American Way... helped this happen." In September 2004, Jimmy Swaggert expressed his disgust with gays by telling his congregation: "...if one ever looks at me like that I'm going to kill him and tell God he died." And on the August 22, 2005 airing of his program *The 700 Club*, Pat Robertson, founder of the Christian Coalition as well as head of both a television network and a university, told his audience that it'd be a lot cheaper for the U.S. to assassinate Venezuelan President Hugo Chavez than start a war with him. "You know, I don't know about this doctrine of assassination, but if [Chavez] thinks we're trying to assassinate him, I think that we really ought to go ahead and do it." Robertson added, "I think the time has come that we exercise that ability."

Lastly, while most are familiar with Dobson's much lampooned run-in with SpongeBob Square Pants, what most don't realize is that, according to Dobson, he never had qualms with SpongeBob. Rather,

Dobson was concerned with the group behind the video, "We Are Family," which used numerous popular cartoon characters in a video aimed at encouraging tolerance. Decrying the organization's "homosexual agenda," Dobson wrote in a letter appearing on his website: "Of particular significance is a so called 'Tolerance Pledge' that appears to complement the pro-homosexual propaganda found within the once available school curricula. The second paragraph of the pledge reads as follows: 'To help keep diversity a wellspring of strength and make America a better place for all, I pledge to have respect for people whose abilities, beliefs, culture, race, sexual identity or other characteristics are different from my own.'"

Proving their intent to return the Christian faith to the Taliban-esque rigidity of the dark ages, Rev. Simpson of CAP says one can quickly witness the zealotry of the Religious Right by visiting some of their websites: "If you go to the Coalition for Revival and read all of their documents, if you go to the Chalcedon Institute with R.J. Rushdoony, and you investigate the connections between the theocrats, Rushdoony's group, and the Alliance Defense Fund, which is the sort of fundamentalist ACLU, you'll see very much what these people have in mind for the ideas of government and how the laws of the nation should be understood. I mean, many of these people are for stoning gays and lesbians; they're for executing adulterers, idolaters, people who don't hold their opinions. These groups have coalesced into some larger groups, like the Coalition on Revival and Chalcedon Institute that are, frankly, quite alarming. These organizations have been there for several decades, they're not new."

Since the days of the earliest Christians, followers have always maintained a variety of beliefs and traditions. Before being crushed by the weight of the Christianized Roman Empire's imperial decrees against non-orthodox views, Christian groups like the Gnostics, Ebionites, Marcionites, and the Thomasines flourished. Today, under the protection of the separation of church and state, Christianity has prospered as never before; differences among Christian groups such as Catholics, Baptists, and Jehovah's Witnesses are accepted without rousing calls for blood shed. The reason such peace continues is because our nation has refused to allow government into the theological debate and, conversely, has refused to allow religion to govern the state. And so today, within the expansive religious title of Christian exist thousands of variations—from rituals to exalted tenets to personal approaches and to the nature of the faith itself. Those Christians who allow for and support the demise of the separation of church and state should prepare for the ominous but definite day when the self-proclaimed Protestant popes of the Religious Right create anew a Christian orthodoxy which calls into question their loyalty to Christ and condemns their faith as heretical.

—Originally published in the Winter 2006
issue of IMPACT press.

Overcoming Antagonistic Atheism to Recast the Image of Humanism

⧉

The current collective membership of American Atheists, the American Humanist Association, and the Freedom from Religion Foundation is less than 25,000 members. That number includes people like me who are members of more than one of these organizations.

In 2003 the total annual revenue generated by American Atheists, the American Humanist Association, the Institute for Humanist Studies, and the Freedom from Religion Foundation was less than $3 million. Compare that figure with the $8 million brought in by the Traditional Family Values Coalition that same year, the more than $15 million Jerry Falwell Ministries earned, or the more than $100 million brought in by Focus on the Family.

So what's my point? Humanists need more than good ideas and great intellect to compete with the behemoth of the religious right for the interest and attention of the American public. With the exception of money, what the Humanist movement needs more than anything is a positive, uplifting message and as much good public relations as can be engendered. The last thing the movement needs is more bad publicity, which it unfortunately never ceases to elicit.

Who then is to blame for Humanism's image problem? The media? The religious right? Yes, but they're only half the answer. The other half is that too many atheists see the freethought and Humanist movement as a revolution for waging war on religion. And, as a result, an epidemic of antipathy has battered an otherwise inspiring veneer.

Many outsiders—both nonbelievers and believers—who might otherwise find a naturalistic, secular perspective or philosophy of life worth exploring, see the fanciful crusade of many atheists to "save" humanity from the "scourge" of religion in the same light they view religious fanatics who zealously seek converts. As scholar and atheist Dylan Evans writes: "There seems to be a widespread tendency among people of all creeds and none to think the world would be a better place if everyone agreed with them." Evans goes on to add that, just as religious fundamentalists do, secular fundamentalists "seem to want to convert the whole world to their own point of view."

As one leader in the freethought community (who spoke on condition of anonymity) pointed out to me, "Our biggest problem in the Humanist movement . . . is keeping atheists who just want to complain about people of faith out of our organization. . . . They join and then get upset that we aren't focused on bashing religion." Alister McGrath, author and professor of historical theology at Oxford University writes that "atheism spawns organizations; it does not create community . . . the community thus created seems to be based solely on distaste for religion."

While such observations overlook the positive aspects of Humanism and the affirmative work of such organizations as the American Humanist Association, McGrath nonetheless diagnoses the movement's most serious internal malady, identifying the contagion that has spread throughout the larger freethought community and must be inoculated from within.

ANTAGONISTIC ATHEISM

Perpetuating the caricature of the misanthropic atheist, several writers not only spew vitriol in the face of believers but also actively advocate the use of ridicule and slander in dealing with them. In the preface of his book *Atheism: A Reader*, S. T. Joshi writes: "Even ridicule of religion is an entirely valid enterprise." Complementing this notion, Eddie Tabash, in an article on the American Atheists website, writes that the future of Humanism relies on its members' ability to bash the beliefs of others: "Establishing the social acceptability of ridiculing the absurdities of religious claims is an integral part of gaining acceptance for secular humanism."

Dr. Timothy Shortell provides another example. Not long after becoming chair of Brooklyn College's Department of Sociology, Shortell fueled the ire of religionists toward nonbelievers by writing an online article entitled "Religion and Morality: A Contradiction Explained. I first learned of it through a report by the Christian news service Agape Press, which reported that the atheist professor had therein described religious people as "moral retards" and had said, "Christians claim theirs is a faith based on love, but they'll just as soon kill you."

Reading this, I decided to investigate the article, expecting to find that Shortell had been misquoted or his comments had been taken out of context. But I was wrong. The article was, to my mind, a tirade of irrational generalizations brimming with fodder for religious fundamentalists. One quotation will suffice. Shortell writes:

> On a personal level, religiosity is merely annoying—like bad taste. This immaturity represents a significant social problem, however, because religious adherents fail to recognize their limitations. So, in the name of their faith, these moral retards are running around pointing fingers and doing real harm to others. One only has to read the newspaper to see the results of their handiwork. They discriminate, exclude and belittle. They make a virtue of closed-mindedness and virulent ignorance. They are an ugly, violent lot.

As anyone knowledgeable about history can show, such assertions dismiss the important contributions of deeply religious social justice leaders like the Reverend Dr. Martin Luther King Jr. and former U.S. President Jimmy Carter. While one is certainly free to criticize specific zealots like Pat Robertson, organizations like Focus on the Family, or movements like the religious right, broad and inexact condemnation of *all* Christians or religionists is irrational at best and intolerant at worst. But some atheists are now arguing that believers are incapable of rationality and that we should no longer exalt the principle of tolerance. In his essay, "An Atheist Manifesto," author and philosopher Sam Harris argues that "the incompatibility of reason and faith has been a self-evident feature of human cognition and public discourse for centuries." Harris goes on to declare "interfaith dialogue" and "mutual tolerance" futile. The only way to banish religious warfare, he writes, is to eradicate "the dogma of faith." Renowned atheist biologist and 1996 Humanist of the Year Richard Dawkins recently went so far as to denounce a progressive Christian, the Right Reverend Richard Harries, forty-first Bishop of Oxford, for betraying reason. Harries appeared in a film by Dawkins, in which Harries outlined his opposition to creationism. After their conversation, Dawkins accuses him of betraying reason "just because I was religious," wrote Harries later. Responding to Dawkins' criticism, Harries penned a column, "Science does not challenge my faith — it strengthens it," in the April 16, 2006 *Observer* in which he points out the irony that those like Dawkins and Harris actually advance the agenda of Christian fundamentalists:

> Indeed, the leader of the American creationists has apparently written to Dawkins to say that they daily thank God for him. The reason is simple. Dawkins argues that evolution inevitably implies atheism. That's what we believe, say the creationists in effect, therefore evolution shouldn't be taught in schools or, if it is, only with creationism taught as well. Creationism and atheistic fundamentalism prop one another up. Each would collapse without the other.

Looking back to December 2005 we can find a good example of how antagonistic atheism helps to prop up Christian fundamentalism. As most will recall, the religious right charged that secularists had declared war on Christmas. Pundits on the right were particularly upset with the decision of political leaders in Boston, Massachusetts, to name the city's annual Christmas tree a "holiday" tree. They also objected to retailers' use of slogans like "Happy Holidays" rather than "Merry Christmas." Most Americans rightly dismissed such rhetoric as silly. But Beyond Belief Media, the group responsible for the film *The God Who Wasn't There*, made the victimization fantasy a reality by actually declaring "war on Christmas." In a December 5 press release, BBM's president, Brian Flemming, stated: "Christian conservatives complain nonstop about the 'War on Christmas,' but there really isn't any such war." He went on to explain that his group chose to wage a real war on Christmas in order "to demonstrate what it would look like if Jesus' birthday were truly attacked."

Flemming's comments were in direct contradiction to those of Joseph Conn of Americans United for Separation of Church and State, who rebuked the religious right's propaganda. "There is no war on Christmas," Conn said. "This is in large part a publicity stunt and a fundraising maneuver by Jerry Falwell." The Reverend Barry Lynn also observed that "Jerry Falwell has found that this war on Christmas is a very good, healthy, fundraising mechanism." But at the start of December, during the Christmas controversy, a group of college students at the University of Texas at San Antonio made headlines with their "smut for smut" event, in which they gave away pornography in exchange for religious literature.

While these kinds of cute spectacles succeed in garnering media exposure, they never fail to play into the religious right's hands by casting atheists in a misanthropic light. The portrait of atheist organizations as hate groups and atheists as people tirelessly plotting to ruin religion or just plain antagonize believers simply feeds the paranoia of the 64 percent of Americans (as determined by the Anti-Defamation League in October 2005) who believe religion is under attack. Despite the fact that the so-called threat to religion is a mostly nonexistent ruse, it's hard to ignore the likelihood that the anti-religious rhetoric of many atheist pundits fuels the religious right's persecution propaganda and helps fill its coffers.

In addition to being strategically unpalatable, antagonistically ridiculing the beliefs of others is seen by many, even within the Humanist movement, as a form of bigotry. Jennifer Hancock, executive director for the Humanists of Florida Association, says:

> [Ridicule] is offensive. It is a form of religious bigotry. When I hear someone say Catholics are stupid, they are talking about people I love and care about, who are definitely not stupid. Plus, if it

happens to someone's face, exactly how are you going to have a good conversation with someone you just told was stupid. I am an atheist, but that is my personal belief. I don't understand why people believe, and truth be told, belief doesn't make sense to me. But I know from my friends and family members that, as wacky as their belief is to me, my unbelief is just as wacky to them. So, the key is to accept that people really do believe what they say they do, and this is a matter of basic respect.

However, some atheists contend that tactics like those used by the smut for smut organizers are precisely what is needed. R. Senatore of the Broward Atheists (Florida), responding to my article, "Atheists Making Falwell's (X-mas) Dreams Come True," which critiques Flemming's war on Christmas and the smut action, writes that it is "time we atheists took off the gloves and brought the fight to the whackos who pray to walls and make policy for the country." Pointing to a recent incident where a Christian woman took offense to his freethinker shirt, Senatore writes: "We can no longer sit at the sidelines lest we 'insult or rile' the good people who are screwing up our world. I do not believe that we need to skulk into the corner, I believe we need to shout that we are the answer to religion and its foolhardy teachings!"

Unfortunately, such attitudes will continue to thwart Humanists in their efforts to make necessary gains in terms of expanding association and membership, forming alliances, and acquiring clout in the community. If we don't look to our commonalities instead of relying on simplistic, dichotomist-style thinking, our treasured U.S. Constitution may be gone before we know it. The truth is that not all Christians feel threatened by freethinkers and many of them—including the Christian Alliance for Progress, are working alongside Humanists to create a better, more rational world.

ANTIDOTE FOR THE ANTAGONISTIC IMAGE

The dilemma, however, remains: how do Humanists respond to fundamentalism's charges and how can a positive image of the Humanist lifestance be promoted. If not via angry, antipathetic activism, then what? Well, a handful of innovative freethinkers have proffered an antidote for this antagonism, an antidote that isn't only more tolerant but much more effective. Earlier this year atheist Hemant Mehta organized a brilliant action which, due to the nature of its openness and good-natured spirit, unintentionally increased dialogue rather than squelched it. Mehta, now known around the nation as the "eBay atheist," decided to auction off his time, pledging to attend church for at least one hour for every ten dollars the highest bidder paid. By the time the bidding ended, forty-one bids had been placed and eBay item number 5660982226 had sold for $504. Winning bidder Jim Henderson, a liberal evangelical seeking to reinvent evangelism, asked Mehta to attend nine church services and write two pieces for his website www.OfftheMap.com.

As part of the deal, Mehta pledged to "go willingly and with an open mind" and to "respectfully participate in service, speak to priests, volunteer with the church if possible, do my best to learn about the religious beliefs of the churchgoers, and make conversation with anyone who is willing to talk. (Though I do reserve the rights to ask the person questions about the faith.)" Mehta's project resulted in a flood of print and radio media attention, not to mention a rise in public interest. Numerous newspapers, including the *Wall Street Journal* and the *Village Voice,* ran headlines like "On eBay, an Atheist Puts His Own Soul on the Auction Block." But rather than fueling outrage, most of the stories brimmed with humility and openness, being accessible to anyone of any faith. Mehta's provocative but respectful action cleared the brush of good-versus-evil rhetoric, leaving a space for rational dialogue.

In a recent interview, Mehta told me he finds negative attitudes and actions such as the smut for smut action counterproductive. Instead, Mehta believes the model set forth by such women as Julia Sweeney and Lori Lipman Brown is the way to go:

> The reason that the eBay thing worked so well is because I think it was a form of positive atheism. It was kind of putting a friendly face out there about it. I actually gave examples, you know when you look at Julia Sweeney's one woman show, *Letting Go of God,* when you look at Lori Lipman Brown from the Secular Coalition for America, they've put a really friendly face about atheists

out there—that they're not out to attack anyone, they just want it to be respected and people to know where they're coming from. I think that's what I tried to model myself after, in terms of how to put this thing out there.

While Mehta visited various churches, atheist Robert Jensen joined one. Jensen, a journalism professor at the University of Texas at Austin, said he joined St. Andrew's Presbyterian Church in Austin as a political act of moral solidarity. In his article, "Why I Am a Christian (Sort Of)," Jensen wrote that his joining affirmed that he: "(1) endorsed the core principles in Christ's teaching; (2) intended to work to deepen my understanding and practice of the universal love at the heart of those principles; and (3) pledged to be a responsible member of the church and the larger community."

Some might think it odd and counterproductive for an atheist to seriously join a church. Had Jensen politely shed his atheism to join St. Andrew's Presbyterian Church, I might agree. Instead, Jensen joined as an avowed atheist, sending a powerful signal to progressive and moderate Christians around the nation: Humanists and Christians have shared and continue to share a number of basic moral values—specifically a love of peace and justice. From whence each derives these values may be different, but the fundamental ethic of the neighbor, of love, is something progressives of all belief systems cherish.

Furthermore, Jensen sees his joining as an opportunity to tear down the walls of religious division. Answering the proverbial question, "Won't expansive conceptions of faith eventually make the term Christian meaningless?" his response is an honest and encouraging "Yes." Jensen says, "The same process could go on in other religions as well. Christianity could do its part to help usher in a period of human history in which people stopped obsessing about how to mark the boundaries of a faith group and instead committed to living those values more fully."

Jensen also asks Christians to consider the potentially nonreligious, universal message Jesus has to offer by asking: "What if the Bible is more realistically read symbolically and not literally? What if

159

that's the case even to the point of seeing Christ's claim to being the son of God as simply a way of conveying fundamental moral principles? What if the resurrection is metaphor? What if God is just the name we give to the mystery that is beyond our ability to comprehend through reason?" He believes that, with "such a conception of faith, a real ecumenical spirit and practice is possible."

The work of atheist biology professor Michael Zimmerman, dean of the College of Letters and Sciences at the University of Wisconsin-Oshkosh, is perhaps the most important and successful in achieving positive results for Humanism while responding to the religious right. A long-time opponent of the teaching of creationism in public schools, in 2004 Zimmerman organized the Clergy Letter Project in which a large number of clergy signed a letter aimed at pressuring the School Board of Grantsburg, Wisconsin, to rescind its alteration of the science curriculum which had given "various models/theories"—essentially creationism—equal footing alongside evolution in public school classrooms. The following year with the explosion of the creation-evolution controversy in Dover, Pennsylvania, Zimmerman decided to take the project national. He said he felt compelled to get further involved in the debate after hearing fundamentalist ministers claim on television that Americans had to choose their faith over evolution. Several months later a new version of his clergy letter, which calls on school boards to uphold evolution and a credible science curriculum, had been signed by more than 10,000 clergy people from a variety of denominations across the United States.

Despite his tremendously successful effort, however, Zimmerman complains that the media paid little attention. "When we hit our goal of 10,000 signatures I thought we would get a lot of coverage," he said. "No one cared. I could not generate almost any interest. . . . I was kind of blown away by that." What angered him the most was that, while his project was ignored by the media, the religious right's mini-crusade to protect the environment received ubiquitous media coverage.

At the same time we gathered those [signatures] the religious right, the evangelicals had a letter signed by, I think it was seventy-eight members of the pretty far right, coming out in favor of doing something about Global Warming. The *New York Times* had a front page story on it and it kind of pissed me off. These are seventy-eight guys and I had ten thousand.

Eventually Zimmerman thought up a second phase to his campaign. He decided to launch Evolution Sunday, a national holiday to be celebrated in churches, commemorating the birthday of Charles Darwin. As proof of progressive Christians' commitment to reason and science, more than four hundred congregations across the United States celebrated the holiday on February 12, 2006. The event succeeded in making headlines across the nation. Zimmerman, who says he's been an atheist for four decades, told me that the only way to protect quality science education in the United States is to work with rationalists within the religious community. "If we don't work with those in the religious community whose values we share, even if we don't share their faith, we will lose," he said. "I think it's just that simple." But, angered by Zimmerman's work, some atheists have accused him of betraying secular humanism and promoting religion. To these critics he responds: "I'm not promoting religion; I'm just making sure that the people who happen to be religious can have good information and can make rational choices. My job isn't to proselytize for atheism. I don't think we gain anything or I don't gain anything by doing that." Moreover, Zimmerman says his support for freethought requires him to respect the rights of others to believe as they wish, so long as their beliefs don't infringe on his rights as a citizen.

Humanists are faced with a choice between two models best revealed by the juxtaposition of Zimmerman and Dawkins. Both biologists hold a profound understanding and respect for science. Both value their atheist viewpoint. But only one is willing to fully and civilly cooperate with believers in the interests of society, desperately in need of a unified progressive movement.

While Zimmerman recognizes Dawkins as "an incredibly bright articulate man" he believes Dawkins views his atheism as "part and parcel of his science. And it's not. . . . It's part-and-parcel of his *be-*

liefs. And he's welcome to his beliefs and he's welcome to criticize anybody he wants. But he's done more damage than help in many ways because of the vituperative quality of his comments."

TO RESOLVE THE DILEMMA

In her August 10, 2005, article "Religion and the Left," *Nation* editor Katrina vanden Heuvel writes: "I believe that one of the key issues facing the left . . . is whether all of us—secular, spiritual, and religious alike—can treat one another with the humanity, honesty, respect and grace we all need and deserve. . . . Can we unite to challenge the religious right through a new politics of the religious left?"

Given the United States' disastrous direction in such areas of concern as torture, inadequate health care, hate crimes, persecution of gays, military spending, poverty, rampant misogyny, and war, we must answer her with an emphatic "Yes!" It's time for Humanists to turn to the wisdom of the Enlightenment once again, recognizing the truth in the words of Voltaire: "It would be the height of folly to pretend to bring all men to have the same thoughts in metaphysics. It would be easier to subdue the whole universe by arms than to subdue all the minds in a single city." Or as Dylan Evans puts it:

> The world contains a dazzling variety of conflicting and irreconcilable worldviews, and this is probably a permanent feature of human existence. The idea that all rational beings will eventually converge on the same point of view, even though they begin from radically different starting points, is a hopelessly naïve view that only holds good in toy worlds such as that of Bayesian epistemology.

Those who defend the crusade to "cure humanity of the pestilence of belief" speak the language of fanaticism and merely invert the argument of religious fundamentalists. Just as we would defend atheism against those who point to its misuses, such as by the former Soviet Union, Christians too argue that particularly vicious Christian rulers have merely molested the spirit of their faith for crooked gains. One would do well to recall that the lesson of the Enlightenment wasn't that the enemy of reason is belief in God. It's that *fanaticism*, be it religious or secular, is the bane of humankind and the

162

true enemy of rational minds.

For freethought organizations to charge ahead with potent, positive, new media campaigns, then, the challenge is to abandon the kind of atheism Evans calls "old and tired." We need to reproach the arrogant atheists for what *New Republic* writer Alan Wolfe describes as "the shrillness of their tone, their thinly disguised contempt for people they can barely understand, and their conviction (you might even call it religious) that they always have been and always will be on the right side of history." In short, we would do well to assail and distance ourselves from any form of fundamentalism, even if it's secular fundamentalism. The sooner Humanists recognize that spiteful antics and attitudes of superiority sadly mirror the presumptive, all-knowing mentality of the religious right and undermine the efforts of organizations like the American Humanist Association, the sooner we can move to grow a vast, vibrant Humanist movement.

—Originally published in the July/August 2006 issue of The Humanist.

CHRISTIAN ALLIANCE FOR PROGRESS PUTS THEOCRATS ON NOTICE

⊁⊀

In a move to save the integrity of the Christian faith and combat the extremist agenda of the Religious Right, a group of Jacksonville Floridians have formed the Christian Alliance for Progress (CAP). The group proclaims unequivocal support for economic justice, gay and lesbian rights, environmental stewardship, reproductive rights, and universal health care.

Before an official launch in Washington on June 22 2005, CAP had attracted thousands of members with virtually no publicity. The organization's arrival on the national stage was received with such enthusiasm that by the end of July 2005, CAP announced that it had about 6,000 new members, swelling the group's ranks to 10,000. Shortly after, the religious fanatical icon Jerry Falwell denounced CAP as, "hardly 'Christian'." He added that the group's "so-called broad-minded efforts toward tolerance have blinded them to how the Bible instructs us to live."

Falwell went on to remind us that Jesus "was not a hippie do-gooder, but rather the Son of the Living God who came to earth to pave the one way to heaven for mankind."[1]

Jerry Falwell, *The Conservative Voice*, "Another Group Arrives to Combat the Religious Right," *July 10, 2005*. http://www.theconservativevoice.com/articles/article.html?id=6805

Reverend Timothy Simpson, CAP's director of religious affairs, said that while he wasn't sure what to expect, he really isn't surprised that CAP has been received with such fanfare: "There *is* a void out there. There are some top down organizations that are populated by fine people, folks that we admire tremendously, but there isn't really anything out here in the hinterland being put together by folks out in the hinterland; none of us are famous, we're just regular people who are fed up." He said the group was formed in part to counter the right-wing pundits and know-nothing talking heads who claimed that all the "value voters" turned out for President Bush in the 2004 elections. "We looked around at our selves and said we're value voters too," Simpson explained, "but we've just got a completely different set of values. We decided we can sit around and grouch about that and complain, or we can do something about it."

CAP organizers also believed that a Christian, Scriptural based response could adequately stand up to the fanatical agenda of radical right pundits like James Dobson and Pat Robertson. "We think that it's very important to counter text by text, scripture by scripture, theological argument and point by theological argument and point, all of the claims and assertions by those radicals from out of the Christian theological tradition," Simpson explained. Contrary to popular portrayal, Simpson says the 2004 election offered a clear indication that millions of Jesus loving Christians across the United States *are* liberals. "(Someone from) the Washington press-core asked me this last Wednesday: come on, this is all nice and everything and you've got a nice press gaggle to cover your little group and everything, but isn't it really the case that Christians, by and large, are Republicans, and support all that? I said... the fact of the matter is that there are tens of millions of people who love Jesus Christ, who love the Church, who love this Country, and who understand the Gospel in completely different terms; and more importantly... they understand that the Gospel is calling us to a different kind of politics." Simpson says it's liberals who most embody the virtues of Jesus. "Liberals try to be the hands and feet of Jesus," he said. "They work the soup kitchens, they work the homeless shelters, they do social justice ministries. The conservatives buy satellites, they buy television stations, they build humongous radio networks."

Among CAP's primary concerns is the Radical Right's work toward establishing a fresh brand of pop-culture theocracy here in the US. Citing historical abuses of the faith by right-wing extremists, Simpson said the separation of church and state is what has protected America from the kind of horror experienced in other parts of the world. Beyond the simple boundaries of left and right wing politics, CAP also seems to be leading a revival of Martin Luther King-styled Christian humanism, countering the Religious Right's mantra of faith over works. Opening the door to interfaith alliances, Simpson says his group rejects the notion that a person has to *be* Christian in order to *share* Christian values. "An atheist that stands with a neighbor," said Simpson, "that stands with poor people; that is concerned about the marginal and the oppressed is somebody who is embodying the values of Jesus. And we will work with them happily in the political sphere on areas of common concern because that's what this is all about."

"Ultimately, in Christian theological terms, the question is: how is the neighbor best served," he continued. "And we want the focus to be on that, particularly the neighbors that are in difficulty, that are in distress, that are in the margins; rather than on trying to get the wealthy in this country another tax cut."

—Originally published under the heading, "Liberal Christian Organization Puts Theocrats on Notice"; Oct 18, 2005, TowardFreedom.com

CONVERSATIONS WITH CHRISTIAN AND ATHEIST ACTIVISTS

⼊

PART I: MICHAEL ZIMMERMAN

As I argued at the 2006 American Humanist Association conference and in articles such as "Overcoming Antagonistic Atheism to Recast the Image of Humanism," progressive secularists and religionists are united in their vision of a tolerant society free of violence, poverty and injustice. To prove it, I conducted four conversations last year with key progressive Christians and atheist activists.

The importance of the lesson of these interviews, that we have more in common than not, cannot be overstated. Why? Because of the mainstream media's insatiable hunger for discord and typological analyses, along with the efforts of secular and religious extremists who continue to undermine and distort this reality.

Most recently, on December 15, National Public Radio did a lengthy story on the rise of what I have been calling "antagonistic atheism." The piece, entitled "Atheist Brigade Takes Arguments to the Tolerant," featured interviews with two of freethought's most controversial and adversarial thinkers, Sam Harris, author of *The End of Faith,* and Ellen Johnson, president of American Atheists. The introduction of the piece says it all: "Now a small group of nonbelievers has a new approach to getting their message out, challenging the faithful with a fiery rhetorical blend of reason and ridicule. Especially ridicule." In the story Brooke Gladstone, host of NPR's *On the*

Media, reported: "Atheism already had a PR problem. Then came Sam Harris, author of *Letter to a Christian Nation.*" She went on to summarize a portion of Harris' comments by saying, "Harris says the only way to win is to keep up the pressure until religious tolerance is no longer tolerated."

Rather than speaking to any number of freethinkers engaged in building alliances, mainstream media outlets continue to foster the illusion of a culture war by crowning vitriolic and intolerant secularists official ambassadors to the broader freethought movement.

Such portrayals create the illusion of a culture war and more particularly, the illusion of a fierce split between long-time allies: religious and spiritual progressives, who have historically worked together to abolish slavery, further women's rights and to crush poverty and intolerance.

Sadly, the media virtually ignores bridge-building projects such as atheist-biologist Michael Zimmerman's The Clergy Letter Project, a statement of support for science signed by more than 10,000 members of the clergy, and the manifesto I co-wrote, "A New Progressive Alliance: A Call for Unity Between Secular, Spiritual, and Religious Progressives," which states the numerous common interests of the three groups.

My own realization of the commonality between progressive believers and non-believers began last year when I spent several months researching the subject. The most convincing part of this research was my frank conversations with key progressive Christians and atheist activists.

Interview: Michael Zimmerman

JN: *What prompted you to take the Clergy Letter Project national?*

MZ: June of 2005 I was in the western part of the state, oddly enough, I had not watched *Nightline* in years. I'm in a hotel and I turn on *Nightline* and sure enough, they have a half-hour show on Dover.... And there were a whole lot of ministers, fundamentalist ministers, who were basically standing there saying, "If evolution is taught in our schools, people are going to hell. And you have to choose, you can't have both; you can't be a Christian and have a belief in evolution, you have to choose one or the other."

Now I know that, in this country we like to believe that most of us are religious people; we are in fact by any statistics, upwardly religious people even though people don't go to church all that much. If you tell people in this country that they have to choose between science and religion, the vast majority of them will choose religion every time, even though they don't know what's going on.

I knew that the dichotomy that was being presented, especially by all these Fundamentalist ministers in Dover and around the country, was simply a false dichotomy. I decided that night that what we really have to do is take the Clergy Letter that was written and circulated in Wisconsin and take it national. I believed if we were able to get about 10,000 signatures we can make an impact.

So we went national, we got our 10,000 signatures, and then decided that wasn't enough. And we declared Darwin's birthday this year, Feb. 12, 2006, to be the first annual Evolution Sunday. And we thought we could elevate the debate significantly beyond what it had been. And we had almost 500, on very short notice, we had almost 500 congregations around the country and some around the world participate in Evolution Sunday. So that's how I got there.

JN: Today we see biologist Richard Dawkins condemning pro-evolution clergy in the U.K., saying they betray reason just because they believe in God. Your work, on the other hand, shows very clearly the possibility of building bridges between Christians and non-Christians.

MZ: Dawkins is an incredibly bright articulate man, the problem is he takes his personal beliefs, he's a proselytizing atheist, there's nothing wrong with that, but it's viewed as part-and-parcel of his science. And it's not part-and-parcel of his science, it's part-and-parcel of his beliefs. And he's welcome to his beliefs and he's welcome to criticize anybody he wants. But he's done more damage than help in many ways because of the vituperativeness of his comments.

In fact, I too am an atheist. And I've been one for 40-years but what I think is important is that we recognize that people can believe what they want, that there are lots of different kinds of worldviews, there are lots of questions that are asked. Science, as powerful as it is, can only answer a subset of the questions that are of critical importance to humans.

Where my rights begin to be impinged are when others begin to dictate, in this country, what's taught in the public schools. That's how I got involved.

JN: *Since you've spoken to so many clergy members who support evolution and science I want to ask you, how do they feel about the relationship between science and religion? And why do you think they're energized by this project?*

MZ: There are two groups. There are the Fundamentalists who are absolutely irate. They believe this project and the clergy who have signed on are all going to hell and they're dragging the country and the world with them. They are the ones who have begun to attack the clergy and attack me personally. The death threats have been mild but they've been there. I don't take any of them seriously.

What's really exciting for me about this portion of the clergy is it allows me to demonstrate clearly that the fight is not between science and religion, the fight is between different religious groups. And this is, whether you teach evolution or creationism is a religious fight. It's not a science fight.

The clergy that have signed the Clergy Letter are very outspoken. And they come from lots of different doctrines, lots of different sects....

They make it clear that there's nothing in their faith that makes them have to turn their back on modern science. That if they have to not believe what they see in front of them, if they have to swear off the experiments and the data from modern science, there's something wrong with their religion. Their religion is stronger than that. They recognize that faith needs to be taken on faith; you don't need scientific data to support their faith.

JN: *Some atheists, along with the most fundamentalist of Christians, are quick to say you can't be both a Christian and believe in evolution. And yet so many do. Talk about the conflict between faith and science as you understand it.*

MZ: Personally, I have no religious faith. I can't get my head around how people can believe in a deity. However, I am perfectly willing to understand that others do. It doesn't work for me, but I have no problem recognizing that it might work for you, that you have different insights than I do. I'm not convinced it's any better than my insights; I'm not convinced it's any worse. As long as you don't force me to accept yours I'm not going to force you to accept mine.

The practical aspect though, is in this country, if we care about high-quality education in general, and more narrowly, high-quality science education, and the attack is coming from the religious right on evolution first and then spreading out from there; if we don't, those who care about, if we don't work with those in the religious community whose values we share, even if we don't share their faith, we will lose. I think it's just that simple.

When the American public is forced to believe or forced to choose between science and religion, they're going to choose religion every time. If we simply say it's science or religion and you have to buy the whole thing or you can't buy any of it, we won't have a science curriculum any longer. So, I think from a very practical matter, and from the liberal perspective of letting people believe whatever they want to believe, without forcing it on anybody else you know, the idea of freedom of thought, and freedom of expression, and freedom of all the things our Constitution requires. Scientists have no choice but to ally themselves with rational people who are members of religious organizations.

—*Originally published January 3, 2007 for HumanistNetworkNews.org*

CONVERSATIONS WITH CHRISTIAN AND ATHEIST ACTIVISTS

⊁⊀

PART II: REV. ROBERT CHASE

Constantly kept aloft by media reports of their extremist views, the religious right presents a monstrous, theocratic visage that terrorizes many freethinkers. As a result, many of us have the tendency to make generalizations about Christianity as if it were a monolithic religion, when in fact the community contains a diverse range of opinions. I once had this tendency, having grown up in a predominantly atheist family that was constantly insulted and fearful of religious mobs taking away our freedom.

The truth, however, is that many Christians want nothing of the portrait of Christianity painted by the likes of Jerry Falwell and Pat Robertson. Progressive Christians share not only freethinkers' concerns over the melding of church and state, but they also share the legacy of having established a clear separation. Christian rationalists such as John Locke, Joseph Priestly and others fought hard to for the division of religion and government. In fact, scholar Isaac Kramnick contends that James Madison and Thomas Jefferson drew from Priestley's writings on the separation of church and state when the two men planned the 1786 statute guaranteeing religious freedom in Virginia.

Christianity is not at all the one-dimensional religion that well-funded ideologues like Dobson and Falwell would have you believe; the 2001 American Religious Identification Survey identified more than 30 different groups under the banner of Christianity. Unfortunately, the diversity of opinions within the Christian religion are not well represented in the media.

To find out more about what more moderate Christians believe, I spoke to Rev. Robert Chase, Communication Director for the United Church of Christ (UCC). Founded in 1957, the UCC has more than 5,000 congregations across the United States, and has about 1.4 million members. Though the religious right would have us believe that all Christians think the same way Pat Robertson does, Rev. Chase explained that vigorous debate is taking place within Christianity over issues such as end-of-life decisions, Biblical literalism, the notion of "true religion" and the value of conversion. He specifically singled out the Terry Schiavo case as an example of the mainstream media's one-sided coverage, presenting the religious right attack as "the" Christian position, when in fact many Christians saw the matter as a private affair.

Interview: Rev. Robert Chase

JN: *How has Christianity changed over the years?*

RC: I think that there are a whole variety of forces and factors both historical and contemporary that shape the way Christianity is viewed across the culture. The biggest concern that I have as a progressive Christian voice or one with a progressive perspective is that there tends to be the view that Christianity is monolithic, kind of like in the 60's all people thought that all blacks thought the same or there was a women's perspective. Often the media will say "the Christian perspective."

I remember when there was the Terry Schiavo case there were the concerned folks lined up on one side and the Christian groups lined up on the other side. And that implies that there's one way of viewing faith within Christendom and nothing could be further from the truth... So there's a wide variety of expressions of faith within the Christian tradition and as it's expressed in our contemporary culture. And so the first thing we'd want to do is disabuse people of the notion that all Christians are cut from the same cloth or think alike or have the same processes or perspectives on how they interpret what's happening the world today.

JN: *Take something like the notion of "true religion" which was largely developed in Rome with the birth of Christianity. From your perspective on the issue of "true religion," do you feel like yours is the only religion that can get you to where people need to go?*

RC: My religion is the only religion that can get me to where I need to go. And sometimes it doesn't even do that too well. I think the notion of claiming a "true religion" is one of the greatest idolatries in the world today and leads to some of the unbelievable violence and chaos that we're currently experiencing. You know when you start thinking "God is on my side" as opposed to "I'm on God's side," perhaps, then you run the risk of putting God in a box that's convenient for you and your perspective or your community or your group or your cause or whatever.... .

JN: *On the point of Scripture, to be a good Christian or to be someone — a part of your church, everyone doesn't necessarily have to read the Bible literally, correct?*

RC: I think the biggest split in the Christian church today, that's capital "C" across all denominations, is the split of Biblical literalism as opposed to a contextual understanding of Scripture. Once you start getting a literal interpretation, I mean you could get crazy about this... there's symbolic language... What we believe is that God speaks to each individual in the context of his or her own life.

JN: *A group named The Rockridge Institute did a 2005 project speaking with a number of progressive Christians. One question the institute put to the participants was: "How do we reconcile 'spiritual progressivism' with 'separation of church and state'?"...*

RC: I'll respond to it two ways, and again using Scripture since that person used Scripture, Jesus' famous saying, "render to Caesar what's Caesar's and to God what's God," I think really calls for a separation of church and state... The old notion of power corrupting, unfortunately, is what occurs frequently and if we are a part of the power elite, we in the religious community, that becomes hard for us to speak truth to power.

I think you're seeing some of that, for example, in the administration today. Some of the justification for some of the policies that the administration has undertaken is on a faith basis or justified as being the way that the president's religion is expressed, and therefore there should be a blurring of the line between faith and civil society. The classic example of how that can be destructive is in the Taliban. I mean there's an example where the civil society and the religious society are one and the same, when there's no check and balance, then extremism is a very real possibility...

JN: Do you feel like the separation of church and state is also necessary to protect groups like yours from the rise of a Protestant orthodoxy that might at some point turn around and say, well you know this UCC group, they're really out of line in many of their views, we need to reign them in?

RC: Right. I think that's absolutely true. In many ways that's what's happening. Our not being able to advertise on some of the networks in terms of our television commercials that we tried to air last year as an example of that. Now that's not the government saying that, but it's kind of that government-media, corporate elite that made those decisions...

JN: Back to the church-state separation question. Can you (give an example of) the difference between a progressive Christian influence informing a person to go into the community and struggle for social justice issues, the difference between such a case and an Evangelical going in and trying to restrict gay marriage or stop passage of hate-crime legislation, or gay and lesbian adoption? What's the difference between them pushing their views and the way that progressive Christians like yourself and your group pushes?

RC: There was a time, as a child of the '60s I recall this well, there was a time when conservative religious folks felt — conservative Fundamentalists, the people who were on what we now call the Religious Right —believed that Christians shouldn't be involved at all in the political machinations of the day. That they should keep themselves separate and that their issues should be solely focused on personal salvation and that kind of thing. It was really the work of the Devil to get involved in the society itself.

Over the past couple decades that's really changed, and its changed radically so that the pendulum has swung to the point where now you have places like in Ohio where you've got conservative churches who are being accused of not complying with IRS statues because of their support for particular candidates and stuff like that. I don't think, in essence, there is a difference, I think that these are individuals with, whether they be left or right, with personal agendas or political agendas or causes that they believe in.

JN: How does a group like yours perceive the rise in alternative religions such as Wicca? And how about working in coalitions with such groups in areas of social justice?

RC: Working in coalitions for social justice would be something that we would be absolutely comfortable with so that I can state categorically. I mean we do that all the time.

JN: Regardless of faith?

RC: Regardless of faith or for those people who do not consider themselves part of an organized faith, or who are atheists or agnostics. We do that kind work in the social justice realm because we believe that there's a call for us to do justice.

You've got to understand, the UCC has a very broad understanding of both personal and congregational autonomy so there is a wide range of belief systems that exist within our denomination... And what we're trying to therefore do is to open our doors, especially to those who have been excluded or hurt by the church.

JN: *I mainly meant a certain acceptance.*

RC: In terms of coalition building, there's certainly room for other faith perspectives because I think many of us feel that an understanding of those faith perspectives enriches; that doesn't threaten my Christianity, it enriches it. And that's how I think many of our folks feel.

JN: *So you're not called to necessarily convert people?*

RC: We've had some bad experience with conversion. The Native Americans would be the first to tell you that. What we try to do is live by example. And, again a lot of this is me talking here, but by the fruits of the spirit people will know what my faith is. If I'm a spiritual person, a sensitive person, a loving person, a grace-filled person, then hopefully others will see that example and seek to emulate it. And that's how I think conversion happens. You leave conversion to God, you do your example.

JN: *Atheist author Sam Harris recently wrote an article arguing "The conflict between religion and science is inherent and (very nearly) zero-sum. The success of science often comes at the expense of religious dogma; the maintenance of religious dogma always comes at the expense of science." Yet Martin Luther King once wrote: "Science keeps religion from sinking into the valley of crippling irrationalism and paralyzing obscurantism." Do you feel religion stands to benefit from an improved relationship via more rational religion?*

RC: For me science is a gift from God. So it doesn't threaten at all... I think that there are fascinating intersections between the world of faith and the world of science. The more I understand science, the deeper my faith because, the bottom line, and scientists will say this too, the bottom line for them is a profound mystery. If we can try to get at the heart of that mystery then we're getting simultaneously at the heart of science and at the heart of God...

JN: *It sounds like that's a big part of a group like yours has to fight against, some of these assumptions about Christian belief that these groups are purporting whereas yours is quite different.*

RC: That's right. And unfortunately in our society today you don't exist if you're not in the media; the media has dumbed down what it means to be a Christian to the point where there is, as I said at the beginning of this conversation, this kind of monolithic everybody-believes-the-same kind of impression of what it means to be a Christian and that just couldn't be further from the truth, especially as its expressed in the UCC.

—Originally published January 10, 2007 for HumanistNetworkNews.org

CONVERSATIONS WITH CHRISTIAN AND ATHEIST ACTIVISTS

>K

PART III: JAMES ROWE ADAMS

In 1994 James Rowe Adams founded The Center for Progressive Christianity (TCPC). According to Adams, TCPC "encourages churches to focus their attention on those for whom organized religion has proved to be ineffectual, irrelevant or repressive." In February 2006, Adams stepped down from the presidency, now serving as an honorary advisor. Ordained in 1958, Adams stepped down in 1996 as rector of St. Mark's Church on Capitol Hill in Washington, DC. Focusing on a progressive vision of Christianity and a concentration on arts education, the church's membership grew exponentially and, at one point, *The Washington Post* called St. Mark's "a citadel of enlightened Christianity."

Among Adams's chief interests is supporting good science. To this effect, he has blasted what he calls "unintelligent design" and "anti-intellectual Christainists," whom he believes receive far more media coverage than they merit. In one of his op-ed pieces, Adams complained of some of his fellow progressive Christians who make the mistake of using metaphorical language upon entering the evolution discussion. He writes:

> Unfortunately, in the midst of the political controversy over evolution, some well-meaning progressive Christians continue to write and speak about God as 'creator,' as if they really believed that God constructed the world and intervenes in nature. They may realize that they are using a metaphor, but to the general public they often sound as if they support the notion of intelligent design.

If you think it's odd that a self-avowed Christian would speak so freely on the subject of metaphor and myth, then you haven't been properly introduced to progressive Christianity. Adams is among those Christians who get about as much air-time as freethinkers; that is, none. Adams' kind of Christians—Shockley terms them "Liberal Christians"—"continue to ignore the more miraculous elements of the Bible and of Jesus' story but maintain their embrace of the Israelite prophetic tradition and the social justice implications of Jesus' teaching and preaching. The real battle will be between the fundamentalist Christians on the right and the progressive Christians on the left." Adams states "I think outsiders tend to be fairly ignorant of the strength and the breadth of the progressive church movement. I still don't know why but the media has ignored this almost completely."

In the interview that follows, I ask Adams the hard questions on the minds of hard-line-humanists and the many alliance-minded humanists who still have trouble with organized religion's bloody history. I specifically asked him to address the separation of church and state, organized religion's history of persecution of women and freethinkers and Christian opposition to sound science. His answers will surprise, inspire, and, hopefully, help humanists to realize an often unspoken bond shared between us and progressive believers.

Interview: James Rowe Adams

JN: How far has the progressive Christian movement come since you started TCPC, one of the first to organize?

JRA: When we incorporated in 1994, no one else was using the term "progressive Christianity," nor did the term "progressive" appear often in political discourse. We chose the term partly because no one else at the time was using it.

We started with a small group at St. Mark's Episcopal Church on Capitol Hill in Washington, D.C. We developed an advisory group of academics, parish clergy and lay people. We opened the conversation to the public at a forum in Columbia, S.C., in 1996.

Currently, we have a mailing list of 3,600 households, and we have 293 affiliated organizations. We have ties with similar national networks which developed after ours in Southern Australia, New Zealand, Canada, Ireland and Great Britain.

JN: In your mission statement it says your organization is opposed to exclusive dogma that limits the search for truth and free inquiry. Where does your dedication to inquiry over dogma come from?

JRA: I think there has been at least a minority of Christians, from the beginning, who have taken that point of view. Karen Armstrong (author of *The Battle for God*) finds this line of open inquiry has been present in most religions at least some of the time with some of their adherents….the big breakthroughs in natural science…were brought forth by people who were ordained clergy or had been training to be ordained clergy.

I think of Henslow, who was Charles Darwin's mentor, who was ordained in the Church of England, an outstanding natural scientist. He was the one who got Darwin his post on the *Beagle* and who catalogued Darwin's findings as they would come back in the big trunks. He was just one among many. That whole emphasis has been there. It's just that it was a minority emphasis and the church hierarchies tended to push them aside or push them out.

JN: Does your organization downplay supernaturalism?

JRA: We're not a monolithic group, even among ourselves, but I think the vast number would certainly de-emphasis supernaturalism or remove it all together. I'm in the latter camp.

JN: *How important is the separation of church and state to you?*

JRA: I think that is one of the greatest strengths of the Bill of Rights in the Constitution itself.... There is no mention of God or religion in the Constitution except in one place where is says you can't make a religious test for office. That's all until you get to the Bill of Rights and then comes Congress shall not make any law approving of religion.

JN: *A group named The Rockridge Institute did a 2005 project speaking with a number of progressive Christians. And it asked, "How do we reconcile 'spiritual progressivism' with 'separation of church and state'?" How would you respond to this question?*

JRA: I didn't participate in the Rockridge conversations for the very reason that I don't think religious institutions should be attempting to influence and let alone control government. Many of my colleagues disagree with me. But for me the issue is that progressive churches should be equipping their congregations to act as good responsible citizens and they should be involved in these conversations but not religious institutions. I was appalled by Jim Wallis' book which was praised by some of the Rockridge people, *God's Politics*. I think that even the name itself is blasphemous.

JN: *What concerns, if any, do you have about the movement of the religious left?*

JRA: I object to those on the religious left's saying, or even implying, that they know the mind of God. I also think they err in supposing that all evangelicals and fundamentalists hold extremist views. As you point out, even the Barna Research Group [an evangelical Christian research group] itself admits that under "Ten percent of born-again Christians truly possess a biblical worldview, which BRG defined as accepting Biblically-derived absolute moral truths." That leaves 90 percent of the born-agains who are open to dialogue, at least on some issues. The move on the part of some evangelical leaders to oppose the government's position on global warming is one example of where cooperation is possible.

JN: *How would you define the proper limits of religious organizations insofar as they engage in the realm of social justice and politics?*

JRA: I would not attempt to make such a definition. I think that religious organizations should be free to make the views of their members known and to ally themselves with others who hold similar views. Organizations that do so, however, are not the sort that I would care to support with my time and money. I think, however, that religious organizations have a responsibility to educate their members concerning social and political issues so that the members individually and collectively can fulfill their responsibilities as citizens.

JN: *On the issue of science and Christianity, atheist author Sam Harris has written that he believes "The conflict between religion and science is inherent and (very nearly) zero-sum. The success of science often comes at the expense of religious dogma; the maintenance of religious dogma always comes at the expense of science." Yet Martin Luther King once wrote: "Science keeps religion from sinking into the valley of crippling irrationalism and paralyzing obscurantism." Do you feel religion stands to benefit from an improved relationship with science?*

JRA: I think science and religion operate in two quite distinct realms. And each has a contribution to play to the wellbeing of the individual in society. Religion is about community building and science is about observation and experimenting and the testing of hypothesis. Nothing in science, as far as I can see, is inherently (opposed) to religion or vice-versa. And there are people in the progressive church movement who are still active in their scientific endeavors. And they do cross over.

One of the young scientists that I met at one of our conferences is an evolutionary biologist. And he said we discover points of contact when we realize we have two things in common. One is a sense of doubt and a sense of awe. You can't be a scientist without doubting everything that's gone before. Two Australian scientists doubted that stress was the only cause of stomach ulcers. And because they doubted they found the microorganisms that caused it. Religious people doubt and that's what takes them on their search. One of my favorite bites about the Bible is how many of Jesus' followers, consistently, are called doubters or those of little faith. That's what we are; always doubting. And then the sense of awe that scientists have with some of their discoveries.

JN: *So here there's a meeting between someone like yourself and the secular critics. But maybe the difference is that you would say it's the institution, it's not the religion's inherent characteristics.*

JRA: I would say that yes. Though I think people have good reason to think because it happened so often and in such degree that there's some flaw in the institution itself. And I would say probably so. But it's looking for the options. Look at the attempts to make a purely secular society like the Soviet Union under Stalin, didn't get any better. That's the only real attempt I think we have that we can look at, where people tried to stamp out religion of all forms.

JN: *One of the biggest criticisms of Christianity is the misogynistic aspects of the Bible itself. What is the argument for keeping the Christian tradition rather than creating a new tradition? Is it that you can't get rid of it, so you might as well reform it? Is it that there's something greater in it that has yet to be uncovered or concentrated on? If you agree that the religion itself, the institution, has largely been responsible for so many of these problems, then why maintain it?*

JRA: I don't think I would go as far as to say it's been responsible for these problems, I think they have participated in these problems. If you look at all world history, men have been trying to put women down for at least 3,000 years everywhere, whatever they claim to be their religion or not-religion. Christians have been certainly no better, and, in some cases, worse.

In most cases, there seems to be, as a sociologist taught me, that in times of stress, people need some way of channeling all of the energy which becomes negative if they don't have appropriate rituals to follow.

The National Science Foundation and the National Engineering Foundation did a study some years ago about how people respond to grief at a time of death. And the people who don't end up functioning very well after are those who have no rituals to follow. They examined thousands of cases and the people who worked through grief, didn't matter if they believed it or not, but if they did a ritual tradition that was traditional in their culture, they could work it through and move out the other side.

The same is true with marriage, the birth of children, to mark two other traditions, and even the Soviets ended up having to invent rituals because human beings can't seem to function well without them.

JN: *Do science and Christianity have to be at odds?*

JRA: I don't think they have to be at odds at all. I don't see any reason for them to be at odds. People are doing good science. I think they have to be accountable for the way they use the science but I think for most of the scientific endeavors the morality is being honest.

Look at this great flood of fake evidence that has been turning up in the news lately. Scientists do not seem to have their moral compass functioning in some areas some of the time. There is a danger in trying to make science itself into a religion. That it doesn't have a tradition of moral examination.

I don't think, in many areas of public policy, good science can tell you the best answer. And we've had many scientists experiencing spasms of conscience about turning loose nuclear energy, for example.

JN: *Do you believe that secular progressives and spiritual progressives across the board can work together again as they had to abolish slavery and fight for civil rights?*

JRA: Yes.

—Originally published January 24, 2007 for HumanistNetworkNews.org

CONVERSATIONS WITH CHRISTIAN AND ATHEIST ACTIVISTS

⋊⋉

PART IV: HEMANT MEHTA, THE EBAY ATHEIST

By now nearly everyone in the secular-humanist community knows Hemant Mehta, AKA the eBay atheist and the *Friendly Atheist*. In 2006, Mehta, an ardent activist in the atheist community, wanted to show Christians that not all nonbelievers are the angry, anti-religious people they may think them to be. So Mehta auctioned off his soul — that is, he allowed bidders on ebay to vie for his time, vowing to spend an hour in church for every $10 donated. By the time it was over, 41 bids had been placed and item number 5660982226 was sold for $504 (which Hemant donated to the Secular Student Alliance).

The winning bidder, Jim Henderson, a liberal evangelical seeking to reinvent evangelism, asked Mehta to attend nine church services and write two pieces for his website, *Off the Map*. For his part, Mehta agreed to attend the services with an "open mind" and to "respectfully participate in service, speak to priests and volunteer with the church if possible." Graciously fulfilling his end of the bargain, Hemant's humble, respectful manner immediately countered the "militant atheist" stereotype supported by the mainstream media to speak on behalf of the broader secular community. His strong but inviting manner resonated in the press coverage he received, helping to cleanse the long-standing visage of vituperative atheism.

By the time all was said and done, Hemant's tour of churches in four states, Illinois, Michigan, Texas and Colorado, had been covered by major news outlets including Fox News, *The Village Voice*, *The Wall Street Journal*, *The Chicago Sun-Times*, *The Seattle Times* and National Public Radio. He even scored a book deal through the Christian publisher WaterBrook Press, which plans to release his book, *I Sold My Soul on eBay: Viewing Faith through an Atheist's Eyes* on April 17. Mehta currently maintains his busy website and is the chair of the Secular Student Alliance Board of Directors.

In an interview I conducted in 2006, Mehta told me he believed it was a waste of time to try to extinguish religion and said freethinkers were better off spending their time engaging in productive dialogue with believers. He pointed to Lori Lipman Brown and Julia Sweeney as having preceded him in proffering the "friendly atheist" image, one he believes is far more productive than the antagonistic models used by those encouraging believers to trade in Bibles for pornography. A new voice for freethinkers, Hemant also believes freethinkers can learn a lot from church communities.

Interview: Hemant Mehta

JN: *What prompted you to auction your time off on eBay?*

HM: It's an idea I'd had for a while, but the main thing is just spending so much time with atheist groups, and my family is very religious, too. I think what happens is people don't want to see what the other side has to offer at a certain point, maybe it's a certain age or a certain time in your life, but at some point you think you've seen what everyone has to offer. And so there's no need to look anywhere else. And I think I hadn't experienced Christianity anyway, so before I got so stuck that, "OK I'm an atheist, there's nothing that's going to change me," I figured, well OK, I'll look into and see what they have to offer. That's the least I could do....

JN: *Were you partly motivated by a desire to create dialogue between Christians and atheists?*

HM: I think if I said yes, it would make me sound better than I am. That wasn't the original intention, the dialogue created. I did want to write about any church that I went to and I did want people to respond to it. But the dialogue that happened as a result was just a great byproduct but it wasn't the original intention.

JN: *What was the response like from the Christian and atheist communities?*

HM: Most of the critiques from the Christians were pretty positive, the ones I've seen just going through blogs. I've seen very little criticism from people who actually knew what was going on....the first time I really talked to an atheist crowd was at the [2006] Kansas City convention for Atheist Alliance International [AAI], and it was unbelievably positive there too....

JN: *What about letters and emails?*

HM: I haven't gotten that much response from atheists through email but a lot of religious people have emailed me. And most of them are positive about it too. Most of them want me to come to their church. Like I got seven Jehovah Witnesses, I got a Mormon, a lot of people saying, "That's nice that you've done this with the Christian churches or those types of Christian churches, now come to mine"....no one's said you're going to hell for doing this, which surprised me.

JN: *Right before you took this up I wrote an article critiquing the approach of Brian Flemming's film,* The God Who Wasn't There *and its "war on Christmas" stunt; and then, at a Texas college, there was*

"smut for smut," where atheists were giving out pornography to people who would turn in their Bibles. Some responded to my article asking, hey, then what's the alternative? Not long after you became the
eBay atheist.

From what you're saying, it seems that your activism was vastly
well-received and managed to create conversation whereas these
other forms of atheist activism created bitter controversy. Based on
your experience what's your impression of these more negative kinds
of atheist actions?

HM: It's funny you mention those other examples because when I did
my speech at AAI, I actually said the reason that the eBay thing
worked so well is because I think it was a form of positive atheism. It
was kind of putting a friendly face out there about it.

I actually gave examples, you know when you look at Julia
Sweeney's one-woman show, "Letting Go of God"; when you look at
Lori Lipman Brown from the Secular Coalition for America, they've
put a really friendly face about atheists out there, that they're not
out to attack anyone, they just want it to be respected and people
to know where they're coming from. I think that's what I tried to
model myself after, in terms of how to put this thing out there.

But I don't care if you convert to atheism. I think the belief might
be wrong but I don't think in principle Christianity is a bad thing or
anything like that. And then I had some examples of what I thought
were bad images for us out there and I actually used the smut for
smut as an example as well as the "war on Christmas" thing.... Just
the way you present it, the smut for smut thing, obviously that's going to get publicity, but it's not positive....what you can do is try to
work with it and find a good compromise. When it comes to issues of
having creationism in school, yes I have an issue with that. But if you
want to believe that stuff on your own terms, that doesn't bother me
so much, except that, well, I don't think it's right.

JN: From your sense of their [church communities] tremendous ability
to produce a positive environment for the growth of a community, is

there a lesson about our need to create that sort of community or community centers?

HM: Yes, if we could create communities of reason or something where it's like a church, in the sense that you have this community, a place to go to where there's a set service every time; and a lot of local groups do try to do that and do it pretty well. But yes, to have something like that where anyone can come into and ask questions and talk about this type of thing. The churches do that better than any place else....

JN: *There are atheist pundits like Sam Harris out there right now who say the only way we will ever find peace on earth is when we eradicate religion from the face of the earth.*

HM: I just got his book and I haven't been able to read it yet. But I know that's his basic premise. He almost respects fundamentalism more than the liberal religion because at least they're sticking to their faith. But we're not going to get rid of religion any time soon, so what you've got to do now is learn to find the commonalities with them and work with them. There are legitimate church/state issues that we'll come across, but you could still work with churches. Churches are not bad places and I think that's kind of the impression you get a lot of time.

JN: *What's the purpose of Friendlyatheist.com?*

HM: The purpose is I wanted to get those two words together....First of all, let's link up the image of atheists being friendly because I don't think they have that notion together, or those words are oxymoronic to them. That's the main purpose, let's get that out there. After that it's just more of a personal website to dialogue what's been going on since the auction.

—*Originally published February 14, 2007 for HumanistNetworkNews.org*

CONVERSATIONS WITH CHRISTIAN AND
ATHEIST ACTIVISTS

⋈

PART V: ROBERT JENSEN, JOURNALISM SCHOLAR

Jensen, Part I: Independent Media and Objectivity

When independent journalists step beyond the corporate media's code of courtly niceties in dealing with government policy and officials, they are often saddled with the label of 'advocacy journalism.' Meanwhile, the incestuous relationships between mainstream journalists and policy makers escape popular scrutiny. Consider Tom Brokaw's comments during President Ford's memorial service earlier this year. In his eulogy, Brokaw made light of how the White House press corps under Ford enjoyed certain "advantages" that "contributed to our affection for him" such as going "to Vail at Christmas and Palm Springs at Easter time with our families." Recently I asked Robert Jensen, an atheist and professor of journalism at the University of Texas at Austin, about the value of independent media, and the question of objectivity in mainstream and independent news.

Dr. Jensen teaches at the University of Texas at Austin's School of Journalism and is the author of several books including The Heart of Whiteness: Confronting Race, Racism and White Privilege, (City Lights Books, 2005), Citizens of the Empire: The Struggle to Claim Our Humanity, (City Lights Books, 2004) and Getting Off: Pornography and the End of Masculinity, (South End Press, 2007).

JN: Let me start by asking about your view on the rise of Independent media and its importance?

RJ: First of all, it's important to realize there have been independent media in the U.S. for decades, centuries probably. For instance, there was once a really thriving labor press, independent labor newspapers. I've heard quotes that there were, at one point, 800 labor papers in the U.S.. So before the digital revolution there was always an independent press. We saw it in the 60s coming out of the counter-culture, alternative magazines, newspapers, that sort of thing. So I think it's important to realize this isn't a new phenomenon. But technology and perhaps political developments have accelerated it. So now, eventually with radio and the low cost of doing radio relative to other mass media and, eventually, of course the internet, there were a lot more options for this. And at the same time that the technology made it easier and cheaper, there was a growing, I think, sophistication about the limits of corporate commercial media. So that comes together.

So what's the importance of it? Well two things. One, obviously, it allows people to get news and analysis directly from independent journalists. That's very important. You know, people talk about going around the filters of the mainstream media so there's obviously the direct provision of information. But there's another affective alternative or independent media that I think is sometimes overlooked; which is that when independent media takes up stories that the mainstream press would otherwise ignore, then it puts pressure on the mainstream media to cover (them). This is occasionally evident in a direct sense. You can see a story that was picked up by the mainstream media pretty much out of the alternative media. But in general it makes journalists more aware, and this is discussed often within the industry, it makes journalists more aware that news consumers have more choices and they've got to start thinking about what people want to read. Now that's not only going to push news in a progressive way, it's also going to push it in a reactionary way, because there's a big chunk of the U.S. population that wants reactionary news; that is, wants news coverage to deepen their own ideological framework and prevent challenges to them. It's a mixed bag in that sense.

JN: *Recently two widely circulated independent magazines went out of print,* Impact Press *and* Clamor Magazine. *Many independent publications come into being for a short time and then sort of dissipate because of financial ruin or some other cause. Do you feel that despite their eventual downfall those kinds of publications are essentially successful?*

RJ: First of all, yes. Sometimes when projects fail in the sense that they don't continue indefinitely people get depressed and they should remember that there are often many, many ways in which those (projects) serve a purpose. One way is that they help bring people together.

For instance, we worked on an independent labor paper in Austin in the late '90s, and some of the connections I made and people I met, things I learned while doing that are still useful to me, valuable to me in organizing. There are all sorts of benefits from any activity that brings progressive people together and we shouldn't forget that. But of course during the time that they exist, they provide that information.

All that said, I think we should be thinking about why those publications so often fail. Some of it is, perhaps, in the cards. It's hard to sustain financially, there's not advertisement revenue, or maybe there's not enough subscriptions, whatever. But I think a lot of the publications that start, start from the wrong position in that they don't have a well thought out, I hate to use the term, 'business plan,' but that's the term.

JN: How do you view your work, being a journalist with a particular aim and set of values, and the challenge of being objective?

RJ: Here I actually differ from a lot of people on the left and people I run into. First of all, I don't label myself as a 'journalist' anymore. At one point I worked within commercial journalism, then I went back to school. And I do write a lot and a lot of what I write ends up in journalistic venues. But I do not consider myself a journalist. I consider myself a former journalist with a certain set of skills who now applies them in the context of political movements.

If this term weren't sort of denigrated I would happily use it, I'm a polemicist. I write political polemics that are designed to persuade people. Now in doing that, I think I do it honestly. I think I'm fair about evidence and logic. In other words, I think I'm a good writer and a reasonable thinker. But I don't pretend to be filling the role of journalists. I'm not a journalist in the industry sense, because I don't think conventional corporate journalism is objective. In fact, I do a lecture where I say the conventions of mainstream, corporate, commercial journalism, that is the news gathering routines that rules about who is and isn't a source, all of that, which are called 'objectivity,' actually produce a very non-objective news in philosophical terms. What I mean by that is journalists adopt a certain set of routines that actually limit their ability to understand the world because it channels them toward official institutions and official sources, which tend to provide them with a very distorted view of the world.

So what I would say is that the goal of journalism is to be independent of other centers of power and independent of movements. I am not. When I write, I write as a member of a movement. A journalist, I think, should write as an independent person. And I think that's important. It allows journalists to investigate and interrogate and think in different ways. So, does everybody have a political opinion? Yes. But one of the jobs of a journalist, in the sort of idealized way I'm speaking of it, is in fact not to simply pursue one's political agenda, but to act as an independent researcher who goes out into the world, tries to understand the world. Yes, one has a political perspective that frames the way one asks questions, leads you to some questions and not others. Clearly people's politics has an affect on how they go forward, but that doesn't mean that one's journalism can be reduced to one's politics.

Jensen, Part II: The Veil of Ignorance, Beyond Religion

Last year, around the same time Hemant Mehta (the eBay atheist) was visiting various churches, atheist and journalism scholar Robert Jensen joined one. Jensen, a journalism scholar at the University of Texas at Austin, said he joined St. Andrew's Presbyterian Church in Austin as a political act of moral solidarity. In his article, "Why I Am a Christian (Sort Of)," Jensen wrote that his joining affirmed that he: "(1) endorsed the core principles in Christ's teaching; (2) intended to work to deepen my understanding and practice of the universal love at the heart of those principles; and (3) pledged to be a responsible member of the church and the larger community." Needless to say, criticism was fierce. The Reverend of St. Andrews, Jim Rigby, was roundly condemned by various Christian commentators.

Earlier this year, I spoke with Jensen about his personal beliefs regarding religion and how he got involved with the church. In response, Jensen challenged freethinkers to open their critical analysis to all potentially corrupt power structures, not just religion. He also urges rational minds to strip away all of their illusions, be they illusions about supernaturalism or societal constructs.

JN: *Are you an atheist?*

RJ: It depends on what one means by the term, it's been developing.
The piece I wrote where I called myself an atheist who is now a Christian was sort of meant to provoke discussion. Here's the point—I just had to answer an email from a guy was telling me I should stop mucking around in the church all the time—I think that throughout human history people have struggled with that which is beyond the human capacity to understand. There are some funda-

mental questions that are simply not answerable through reason and science, a whole bunch of them actually, obviously. And one of the ways that people try to understand all of that mystery is through what we call religion. Now when religion gets calcified into rigid beliefs that there are forces outside of ourselves that direct us and that we have to sort of bow to those forces that take a kind of human form, either through an anthropomorphic god or organized religion. I think that's very counterproductive. And in a post-Enlightenment, post-scientific revolution world, it's actually rather silly. But if religion and the stories that come out of religion, the myth, the poetry, the parallels, the lessons, if those can be understood as that ongoing human struggle to understand that which is beyond us, and convey those in a way through ritual and story that are meaningful to people, well, then I'm a religious person.

But in traditional terms, yes, if you ask me do I believe in a God as a force or a being, no; do I believe that Christ was resurrected and rose from the dead, no. But I do believe that religion is a vehicle that, if we can sort of turn it in this direction, is important. It's an avenue I'm willing to explore. It may turn out that, you know, eventually I think it's hopeless, and give it up. But for the time being I think it's very powerful and will continue along that line.

JN: *Shortly after 9/11, you criticized America, citing our nation's foreign policy as equally evil as the acts of the suicide bombers. (I know you also came under intense scrutiny.) Some that are part of the secular-humanist/atheist movement seem convinced that Islamic terrorism or terrorism rooted in the Middle East is simply motivated by nothing short of religious zealotry and hatred of the West. I wonder if you feel that those with an aversion to religion equal to the aversion some fundamentalists have for secularism, become ripe to fall into what some might think is a simplistic analysis of the issue?*

RJ: Just my experience talking to people is that being a critic of religion and making the atheist turn doesn't guarantee one is sophisticated in one's political analysis. You hear all sorts of what, to me, are really very superficial and thin analyses of how the world works from people on all fronts. I mean, I hear religious people who don't seem to care about dealing with facts and complex analysis.

I think, underneath your question is a kind of disappointment that people who are willing to subject one of the fundamental belief systems, religion, to an intense scrutiny and willing to call it out for its failure, are unwilling to do the same thing to the concept of the nation state, especially their own nation state. And I think that's true.

My own political project has sort of been, slowly over time, because I'm not very bright and it takes me a long time to do these things, to look at the fundamental structures of power and the institutions through which they work and ask: is this consistent, when we look honestly, when we look in the mirror honestly, which, you know, is difficult; is it consistent with our best articulation of principles of justice, equality, dignity? And to my mind, every major institution we live in comes up short. Certainly the organized church comes up woefully short. The nation state, especially the United States that at this moment is the imperial power, comes up short. The corporation and capitalism comes up short. More systems like patriarchy and white supremacy, which aren't the same as capitalism and the nation state but are the structuring systems of our consciousness and many of our institutions, they come up short obviously. So I think principled people should apply the same scrutiny to all of the systems they live in. And I think if we do that we get really depressed and we drink a lot — I'm just kidding —, because they all come up short. This is what's hard for people, I think.

If you look around there is nothing, I think, in what we might call the conventional society that holds out much hope. You know like people want to do Green capitalism, they say, well if we can just get capitalism on board with sustainability... My point is that capitalism is fundamentally at odds with sustainability. Then they say, well you know if we could just appeal to American values. What American values? It's a stripping away of illusions that I understand is very painful, because I've gone through it and I still go through it. Every once and a while, I get caught short realizing I haven't gone deeply enough, but that's what we have to do. Religion is one of them, all these others are equally open to critique.

JN: Talk about your motives for joining St. Andrew's Presbyterian, a church in Austin, TX.

RJ: Like a lot of things in life, it's not part of some grand strategic vision I laid out ten years ago. It's a product of who you meet and how you're moved by the world. In this case, the story is very simple. The pastor at St. Andrew's, Jim Rigby, is really quite, I think, an exceptional person. He's both extremely bright and critical and self critical, doing interesting work theologically, as well as politically. He's well known in Austin for his defense of gay rights, risked his own ordination on that issue. So after 9/11 I think he sent me a note saying, hey I liked your piece. And I said, well, hey I like a lot of work you did. We had lunch. A friendship develops. He invites me to do political programs at the church, giving over the church space to an explicitly progressive political agenda, which is rare. It's hard to find. It's actually hard to find an overtly left point of view into the church. You can do nice liberal discussions and things but there aren't a lot of seriously left ministers in this country, in conventional churches. So eventually he invited me actually to preach, using the term loosely, on a Sunday. And all of this built on trust. It's built an intellectual dialogue and a political dialogue between not only me and Rigby but me and other members of the church.

I got to know people on the social justice committee, and then at some point it seemed to me: this is a church that doesn't attempt to narrow and calcify the discussion of spirituality, but is really trying to broaden it out. That's an important part of any progressive political agenda at this point in history, I think. So almost as a sign of my commitment to being part of the community I thought it was important to join. And Jim was willing to allow me to fashion the vows that you say when you stand up in front of the congregation in a way that was consistent with my beliefs, so I wouldn't have to, you know, lie to join the church. And it was, I thought, a natural evolution of my involvement of the church, with church members politically. And I think it's a reminder that, a lot of us are looking for a place to root in community; and it's a culture that is so fragmented and so isolating that to some degree we've got to create community where we can, often in very new and creative ways. But I think we shouldn't turn our backs on those institutions that are good at community building. And churches are good at that. Sometimes in ways that are too exclusive and to exclusionary, obviously, but the struggle is to build on what's positive in the church both theologically and institutionally and avoid replicating all of the ugly elements of the church.

JN: *Do you feel that your political involvement in the church violated the separation of church and state?*

RJ: I don't mix any church activities with state. My values inform my politics, as is the case for all people, whether those values are religious or secular. I find the secular claim that organizing through churches is somehow a Constitutional issue to be odd. I engage in political activity through secular organizations and a church. None of it seems inappropriate in a democracy. Church/state separation is a concept involving government policy.

This two-part interview was published by TowardFreedom.com. Part I was published on December 12, 2007. Part II was published December 24, 2007.

CONVERSATIONS WITH CHRISTIAN AND ATHEIST ACTIVISTS

>+<

PART VI: REV. TIMOTHY SIMPSON, CHRISTIAN ALLIANCE FOR PROGRESS, A CALL TO ACTION

On February 8, 2007, I interviewed Rev. Simpson, Christian Alliance for Progress Interim President, to learn more about his organization's strategy and efforts. It turns out that Simpson is working to not only confront the Religious Right, but also to challenge liberals to become more involved in the struggle for peace and justice.

Rev. Simpson is a minister in the Presbyterian Church USA, holds degrees from Liberty University, University of Florida, Columbia Theological Seminary, and Union Theological Seminary–Presbyterian School of Education. He is also Editor for the Journal of Political Theology.

JN: Rev. Simpson, I understand that you're saving up your money to go to the Christian Peace Witness for Iraq event on March 16-17 (2007) in preparation of possible arrest. What's that about?

TS: We're going to have a worship service at the National Cathedral, then we're going to march down Wisconsin Avenue to the White House and we're going to have a vigil at the White House. And we hope that there will be many hundreds of people, especially many clergy with their ecclesiastical collars on who will get arrested there at the White House, engaging in civil disobedience. Right there at the anniversary of the war. And also during the Christian season of lent which is the time where Christians do repentance and reflection in preparation for the week of the passion, which is the death and resurrection of Jesus, which comes at the end of lent. It's a time of renunciation and repentance where a lot of times Christians will make some kind of personal vow of renunciation so that during lent (people say) "I won't eat any chocolate or I won't eat any ice cream." It's just a reminder of our shortcomings and our need to mitigate our desires which impinge on other people's rights and liberties. What we're encouraging people to do is, instead of giving up chocolate for lent or ice cream or something like that, to instead come and get arrested. Potentially give up your freedom and to bare witness of the immorality of this war that has been done in the name of Christians by Christians, against people of another faith. We really want to frame it in theological terms because we think that our faith has been hijacked by some bad actions.

JN: Where do this war with Iraq and the potential war with Iran stand on the CAP's list of priorities?

TS: Right now it's the most important thing. We're working literally night and day.

JN: How has CAP done in getting its message out?

TS: It's a mixed bag. Sometimes it works very well. Sometimes it doesn't. We got good coverage in September when a number of us got arrested at the Hart Senate office building. I was on CNN, and the *Washington Post* and *Baltimore Sun* were all there interviewing us. My wife was eating lunch at the hospital, where she works, in the break room and all of a sudden, I was on CNN and they were hand-cuffing me and carting me off. That was wonderful. Then there are other times where we do things that don't get any coverage at all. We don't really have an answer for why that occurs.

For the controversy over the *Left Behind* video game, I was on every major network. I was on two different talk shows on the BBC world service. It went viral. It was all around the word. I was on Fox, ABC, CBS, NBC. I had news crews on my front lawn. I was inter-viewed by Reuters, the AP. All about a video game. I don't get that. We didn't do anything more than what we do for other stuff. But for some reason the press fixated on that and that was the story.

JN: On this issue of the Left Behind: Eternal Forces game. When this game came out, some in the secular community pointed to it and said, here come the fanatical Christians again. And yet your organization puts out a press release condemning the game.

TS: We weren't trying to advocate censorship. We were trying to ad-vocate self-censorship for the internal Christian community to not make an ass of (itself). (If) you see somebody in the atheist commu-nity who is standing up bringing scorn on the rest of the community by taking the most absolute extreme position possible that you know is going to set your movement back years; you're not calling for cen-sorship when you stand up and try to shout that person down. You're trying to let the rest of the world know that this crackpot does not speak for the rest of the atheist/humanist/freethought community.

That's what we were trying to do, especially to Muslims around the world. If you live in Saudi Arabia or Pakistan, this video game confirms what the Osama bin Ladens' of the world are saying about American Christianity, that there are people that are making a buck off of training American children that God wants them to whack their non-Christian neighbors. And what I wanted to say to these people was please do not confuse this money making enterprise with the gospel of Jesus Christ and please don't confuse it with the followers of Jesus Christ because the followers of Jesus Christ don't want anything to do with this.

JN: *Do you know anything about the specifics of the game?*

TS: I've been up to my eyeballs. I've been in multiple conference calls with the founder of the company who's been trying to shut me up and who's trying to do everything he can to lean on me to keep quiet about it.

JN: *Can you talk about it?*

TS: First of all, (the founder) tried to appeal to me as a "Christian brother." And didn't I think that this game was a positive thing and because it wasn't Grand Theft Auto or Doom or Duke Nukem or some of those really heavy violent video games where they're rated M and there has been copy-cat things where kids have actually gone out and tried to replicate, in reality, some of the stunts that they saw?

What you have to do in the Left Behind game is constantly click the pray button, especially after you kill somebody, because it causes your spirit score to go down every time you kill somebody. But then you click the pray button and it makes your spirit score go back up. What he's saying is that well, what we try to send out is the message that killing does have consequences. If you are a cold-blooded, brutal killer in this game you will lose. That is the balancing act that you have to negotiate in the game, your killing has to be mitigated by the amount of time you spend in worship.

I said that that was an extremely nefarious thing to be teaching a kid. That that's actually worse than Grand Theft Auto because it teaches Christian kids that, yeah, there are consequences if you kill but all you need to do is just do a little prayer, a little worship and you're good to go and you can whack somebody else. I'm a dad. I don't want my kids playing anything like that. I'd rather them play Grand Theft Auto. I don't let them play Grand Theft Auto — I don't think it's healthy.

[In *Left Behind*] you've got snipers, you've got tanks, you've got helicopters. That this life of violence can just be interwoven with prayer and worship to make it all nice I think flies in the face of the message and teaching of Jesus. I want to say that in the Christian community as well as to secular folks and especially to Muslims who are thinking about coming and blowing themselves up because they see this kind of Christianity as a threat to their way of life. And I want to say we're not a threat.

JN: *Some say Liberal Christians have always been around but are simply underrepresented in the media. Do you feel that CAP is succeeding in opening doors and that more people are realizing that there are Christians who are liberal, that liberalism and Christianity are compatible?.*

TS: It's a very slow process because you're competing against people who own satellite networks. And who, at the flip of a switch, can broadcast themselves. What we're up against is trying to go out and sell ourselves to the *AP* or *Reuters* or to CBS or to some producer for CNN, which is enormously exhaustive, time consuming, and hit or miss, based on the whimsy or whether it's a slow news day or whether or not you get the message absolutely right. So the difference between what they're capable of doing and what we're capable of doing is still a David and Goliath kind of scenario because they have got so much money because they have wedded themselves to the economic policies of big business interests so they have an unlimited supply of funding into which they can tap to get their message out. Whereas we represent the 45 million people who can't afford health insurance or the 1 percent of the American population that's gay. That kind of economic disparity, then, is replicated in a media disparity. But it's more complicated than that. There are other factors.

JN: *Such as?*

TS: Most people on the left, probably 40 percent, think that religion is kind of a private thing. Like you've belched in public, like you've committed a faux pas if you talk about these kinds of things publicly.

What you're supposed to do is hold these things in the quietude of one's heart, which no evangelical believes. But a good percentage of theology left do: my personal beliefs are between me and God. I try to do random acts of kindness. I'm nice to my neighbor. And when I go and vote at the ballot box, I always vote for the liberal things.

But in terms of organizing, putting a bumper sticker on, coming to a rally, writing a letter, the number of those people on the theological left is still quite small. There are tens of millions of liberal Christians, probably less than half are people who really want to do it. They get very anxious by people like me. I know because I hear from them. They say, don't you think you're just becoming a left wing Jerry Falwell. No, I'm not. Jerry Falwell is standing with the bankers and stock brokers and I'm standing with poor people and the drag queens and the homosexuals that everybody else picks on and wants to beat up at the local high school.

JN: How important is it for progressive secularists and Christians to make that commitment, to get out in the streets, to put a bumper sticker on a car?

TS: In a democracy that is a media-driven democracy, it doesn't just happen. Political events are manipulated by a media that is largely controlled by the business class, by the wealthy interests that have the Religious Right in their pocket. The people on the left can have all of these noble ideas in the quietude of their hearts and in their prayer closets and God bless them. But that is never going to transform society. It's never going to ameliorate the conditions of the poor, the oppressed, the marginalized which they ostensibly claim to want to aid. I want to light a fire under my liberal brothers and sisters on this side of the faith community and say, we've got to get out there because we've been getting our but kicked for the last 30 years. If we really believe these things it may mean sacrifice.

I preached at a UCC (United Church of Christ) church congregation this past Sunday that was probably 50-percent gay and lesbian. And that was my challenge to them at the end of the sermon.

(I said) you can sit on the sofa every week and tisk, tisk at the Bill O Reillys and the Sean Hannitys, and you can sit there in your smug self righteous thanking God that you're not like Jerry Falwell or Pat Robertson; or you can get off your butt and do something about it. That all of the sitting there and feeling self righteous that I'm so glad I'm not like those people... those people are out doing something. Those people are on the phone organizing right now. They're raising money. They're planning next week's television show and next month's press conference and tomorrow's radio broadcast to completely destroy your world.

JN: *Given that this is a democracy do you feel people need to realize that they have a responsibility to be more involved in molding society?*

TS: I think it's more than the fact it's a democracy. I think that it's a media driven culture where images create reality and that you have got to get a hold of the images. If you can not get at the images you can not shape the reality that is fed to the people in the democracy. This is not the Lincoln Douglas debates of 1856 where we're gathering together for four hours of debate and discourse over the larger issues of the day. You're getting seven second sound bites from politicians who've been sitting with media advisors all day long preparing for those seven seconds. If the theological left does not learn from that and does not integrate into that reality that we are existing in, the theological left will be left in the dust. And will be left having no place as it largely has come to have no place in shaping matters of public policy.

JN: *How many people are currently involved in your organization, are on your email list?*

TS: 13,000.

JN: *On January 15 2007 the San Francisco Gate published an article, "Writings Show King as Liberal Christian Rejecting Literalism." The piece goes on to discuss a new collection of his works that show him not only criticizing injustices perpetrated by the church but they also show, according to the article, that King didn't believe the story Jonah and the Whale was true or that John the Baptist actually met Jesus and he even referred to the Bible as mythological and also doubted whether Jesus was born to a virgin. Do you feel this Christian liberalism of King's is representative of many other liberal Christians?*

TS: Sure. I think that that's boilerplate liberal, progressive Christian theology and has been for some time.

JN: This theological perspective seems relatively unknown to many secularists and Christians. It seems to me that if you ask most people on the street that they would absolutely think it's insane to have the sort of views where you call yourself a Christian but don't believe almost everything in the Bible actually happened. 'How can you be a Christian if you don't think Jesus was born of a virgin?,' they would probably ask.

TS: That's because they've drunk the kool-aid that Falwell and Robertson and all the TV preachers have sold them. That even secular people—I dare say most of the secularists that will read your article will have read your article—will have drunk that cool-aid, and will have assumed, because that's what they saw on television, that that must be what all Christians believe. And what I'm saying is that's also what they believe in Saudi Arabia, which is why it's so dangerous if liberals don't speak up. We need to let the rest of the world know that the crack pots in the Christian church don't necessarily speak for everybody. They're just the only ones on TV. You've got to make that distinction clear about Christianity and the Christianity that's on television because they're not contiguous.

JN: How do you think Richard Dawkins' book, The God Delusion, will affect or is affecting movement building compared to atheist biologist Michael Zimmerman's efforts as founder of the Evolution Sunday, whereby churches across the United States celebrate Darwin and evolution? Both have the same religious perspectives in that they are not religious at all, and yet they're going about making change in the world in very different ways.

TS: See, I don't think that Dawkins is making change at all except for creating enemies. I think that he's gotten notoriety and I think you have to distinguish notoriety from transformation. On the other hand Michael Zimmerman is bringing about transformation because he is presenting things in a way that faith communities can embrace his understanding of science, which is really what he wants.

Dawkins is driving people away. Fundamentalists will be scaring their children with Dawkins for decades to come. Dawkins is doing his cause no good in Middle America which is who he wants to mock most especially for their superstition, by his tone and the rhetoric. I would agree with him on the science. And yes. Is there any evidence for God? I don't think so. Not in the way that science construes evidence. But people of faith have a whole other set of evidentiary criteria that are not explicable or assailable by scientific method. You either buy that by faith, or you don't as Dawkins doesn't. But making fun of it does not in any way result in having the kind of embrace of the views that he wants people to inculcate into their thinking, which I think that they really need to do. Even as a Christian. I think much of what Dawkins has to say is useful, serviceable, but it comes in a package that is offensive, that is so irritating to people of faith that it's noxious; as opposed to the way Michael Zimmerman is doing it, which is presenting it in a kind scholarly fashion; respecting people; inviting them to bring it into their faith tradition. Not mocking them.... Zimmerman invites people to embrace this scientific perspective as a part of their faith, which, to me, makes far more sense.

—For more information go to ChristianAllianceforProgress.org
or Rev. Simpson's website, www.publictheologian.com.

GIVING UP THE ANGRY HUMANISTS
WHO HOLD DOWN OUR MOVEMENT

✋

When my interview series, "Conversations with Christian and Atheist Activists," surfaced in the *Humanist Network News* Martin White of Salem New York authored a letter to the editor titled, "No More Religious 'Progressives,'" aiming to put an end to the online-zine's inclusion of my interviews. Mr. White believed that I simply want "to curry favor, unite, be subservient to 'religious progressives'" and that he has "no such interest in betraying humanist principles for the sake of illusory bonding."

As a freethinker in the broader application of the term, that is one who applies critical thought and reason to a host of issues, I find logic such as that displayed by Mr. White frightening and all too familiar. Firstly, it is ever important to realize that the Christianity of the 18th century is over. My interviews with progressive Christians show that Christianity is far less monolithic than fundamentalists and the mainstream media would have us believe. Many Christians approach scripture with skepticism equal to that of an avowed atheist. An enormous number of Christians do not believe in the literal word of the Bible, accept evolution and sound science, and reject the divinity of Christ and so forth. In fact, a recently released collection of Martin Luther King's writings indicates that he doubted Jesus was born of a virgin. The straw enemy of the past is no more. Yes, there are still fundamentalists who ignore reason and we must combat such ignorance as best and well mannered as possible. But we should not allow the religious views of a minority of Christians dominate and ill-inform our perception of an enormous percentage of Christians, many of whom are hungry for the same kinds of reform Humanists desire.

Humanists must beware of insisting on unanimity of thought. Our nation currently finds itself in a foreign policy debacle with most of the world viewing us as the greatest purveyor of violence, led by a man who thinks diplomacy is an all or nothing game — "you're either with us or against us." Coming from the rather unique position of having grown up in a large family of atheists – father, brother, aunts and uncles, cousins, grandparents are all atheists–I am the last person aiming to betray "humanist principles." My intention for speaking to religious progressives has not been to undermine Humanism, but to improve our understanding of the people whom we think we are at total odds with. The purpose of the series was, simply stated, to create a dialogue between two groups of people, progressive Christians and Humanists, who do not know each other nearly as well as they think they do. This much is attested to by Hemant Mehta, other wise known as the eBay atheist, who spoke to me at length about how his experience put a human face to a rather alien group of people called "Christians."

One of the most important things for Humanists to accept is that people's opinions, for better or worse, matter. Scientific truth is powerless without a broad base of supporters to support it. Global warming is the perfect example. To accomplish anything in a democratic society, one which permits difference of opinion and belief, one needs to build alliances and create movements.

When I gave a talk at the 2006 American Humanist Association conference on the need for Humanists to put an end to antagonism and put greater effort in building bridges with religious and spiritual progressives, I was surprised at the response. Whereas many of the commentators, both in print and on TV, reflected what I felt was a negative image of secularists, the vast majority of a rather packed room were standing up in applause. If so many people favored bridge-building to name-calling, why wasn't this reflected in the media?

The truth is that angry Humanists are in the minority. And for too long have they have elbowed their way through the room, raising their voices over calmer voices of reason. I for one think they have created a low ceiling under which our movement can grow. The time to give up angry, vitriolic, negative Humanism is now. If we don't, no one should be surprised that we fail to grow.

For me, the first and foremost commandment of Humanism is to make the here and now a better place for as many people as possible. I'll work with and talk to anyone to accomplish that end.

—A significantly edited version of this piece was originally published
April 4, 2007 for HumanistNetworkNews.org

A NEW VISION FOR FREETHOUGHT:
REACHING OUT TO FRIENDS IN FAITHFUL PLACES

⨯⊱⊰

I confess that histories are replete with religious wars: but on close examination, it is apparent that they were caused, not by a multiplicity of religions, but by the spirit of intolerance that ran rife in the religion that considered itself dominant.
—*Baron de Montesquieu (1689-1755), Persian Letters*

For more than a century, American atheists have dreamed of immunizing the world to the pestilence of religion, and its inquisitional horrors. It is this fanciful dream, which implies that all religions are insidious, however, that has hindered, and continues to imperil the future of the Freethought movement. Rather than working to secure the right to not believe within the framework of the United States Constitution's guarantee of religious freedom, Freethinkers have frequently proven more interested in stereotyping and ridiculing religion, and evangelizing universal antipathy towards all religious belief. Such antagonism and righteous hubris has marginalized the movement and alienated potential allies, including secular and moderate religionists. Not only have Freethinkers often aided fundamentalists in identifying atheism with maliciousness and extremism, they also stand as an impotent defense against the brawny religious radicals who continue to besiege the wall between God and government.[1]

Now, more than ever, atheists must rethink the aims and purpose of the Freethought movement. In order to preserve the monumental achievement of the Founding Fathers, Freethinkers must leave the proselytizing to the priests, and make securing the right to think freely their primary purpose. In order to preserve the freedom to not believe, they must defend the First Amendment's separation of church and state and freedom of religion, above all else. To save the wall incarcerating the inquisition of the past and the billowing flames of intolerance bequeathed to the twenty-first century, nonbelievers must: first, acknowledge that they have insufficient numbers to protect the wall alone; second, seek alliances with the millions of religious Americans who respect freedom of conscience and freedom of religion; and third, retire their often uninformed, caustic crusade against the whole of religion, concentrating our criticism, instead, as Voltaire and Thomas Jefferson did, on fanaticism, intolerance, and those who abhor progress, science and reason.

One of the primary reasons the Freethought movement has been unsuccessful in repelling the Religious Right's assault is that there are too few atheists in the United States to mount a formidable defense, alone. Though some tout the findings of the 2001 American Religious Identification Survey (ARIS), which shows a dramatic increase in the number of people who identify with "no religion," many atheists have made incorrect conclusions about the study's findings.[2] For instance, after the release of the 2001 ARIS, the

---

1. Today, the Freethought movement stands paralyzed as religious radicals ravage the First Amendment: Christian-based abstinence only policies strangle common-sense sex education; religious zealots rob women of reproductive rights; creationism challenges evolution in the classroom; for the first time in our nation's history, a governor signs legislation into law in a church, before a specifically Christian audience; the secular institution of marriage is defined as a religious institution, admitting only men and women to wed; the federal government pays out millions of dollars to religious groups, which are permitted to practice discrimination in the hiring process; members of Congress introduce the "Constitutional Restoration Act of 2005," which, if put into affect, would put God in the Constitution among other things. For more information, see http://shelby.senate.gov/legislation/sponsorlegis109.htm.
2. Dr. Ariela Keysar, *American Religious Identification Survey* (New York: The Graduate Center of the City University of New York, 2001), exhibit 1. See appendix 1.

American Atheists (AA) reported that the "ARIS count now shows that the *non-believer* (emphasis mine) population has grown to 29.4 million, roughly 14.1% of the American community."[3] Contradicting this conclusion, however, ARIS study director, Dr. Ariela Keysar wrote that "[i]t is more accurate to describe (the majority of "nones") as unaffiliated than as non-believers."[4] Among the less talked about findings of the ARIS is that 45 percent of the "nones" "strongly agree" that God exists; only 21 percent disagree, and of these only 12 strongly disagree.[5] At best, these numbers show that only about one-fifth of the "nones" are skeptical about the existence of God—about six of the approximately thirty million. And based on the fact only 12 percent of all "nones" *strongly* disagree with the notion that God exists, one can safely conclude that about 2 percent of the entire population is truly atheistic. Supporting this statistic, the 2005 Associated Press/Ipsos Poll of religious attitudes found that 2 percent of Americans "don't believe in God."[6] Still, Freethought organizations like AA frequently misconstrue being without faith in a particular creed to mean a person does not believe in God. Referring to the ARIS survey, AA even reported that among those who identified with "no religion," there are likely "numerous 'closet Atheists' lurking in other labels, using these terms of political or social camouflage."[7] The reality, however, is that professing no particular affiliation with a religion is very different from proclaiming oneself to be an atheist.[8] In my own research on this subject, I found that atheists/agnostics, on average, described their religious belief as rigid, 2.75 on a scale of 1 to 5 (5 being "very flexible"), whereas "nones"

---

3. American Atheists, "Survey Indicates More Americans 'Without Faith,'" http://www.atheists.org/flash.line/atheist4.htm (accessed 5 June 2005).

4. Dr. Ariela Keysar, "No Religion: A profile of America's unchurched," *Public Perspective* (January/February 2003) : 32. See appendix 2.

5. Ibid.

6. AP/ Ipsos, "Religious Attitudes" Poll (June 2005), http://wid.ap.org/polls/050606religion.html (accessed 9 June 2005). See appendix 3. Moreover, a Pew Research Center poll, "Religion A Strength And Weakness For Both Parties," conducted in July 2005, found that 3 percent "don't believe in either" (God or universal spirit/higher power). From Questionnaire Part 2 http://people-press.org/reports/print.php3?PageID=991.

7. American Atheists, "Survey Indicates More Americans 'Without Faith.'"

8. According to the ARIS, only .4 percent of those surveyed called themselves atheists. In comparison, .5 percent of those surveyed identified themselves as Buddhists. See appendix 1.

considered their religious beliefs very flexible, averaging 4.65.[9] In tandem with their flexibility, comments made by "nones" seem to illustrate an openness to spiritual and religious experience lacking in most atheists: One person wrote, "My beliefs are eclectic and would not fall under any denomination that I am aware of. I would say that I am not part of any 'organized' religion so to speak."[10] Another noted, "I have no religious denomination... You could say I believe in my own (religion)." [11] In many ways, one might safely deduce that "nones" are as likely, if not more so, to turn to an alternative religion as they are to turn to atheism.

Even if we were to reject the findings of such respected polls on American religious thought, one sure way to gage the size and efficacy of the movement is by looking at the number of people affiliated with Freethought organizations. A quick turn to the number of atheists who actually belong and contribute to some of the best known national atheist organizations simply confirms the conclusion that Freethinkers can not challenge the agenda of the Religious Right alone. As of June 2005, AA president Ellen Johnson, said her organization has 2,200 members. According to Annie Laurie Gaylor, co-president of the Freedom from Religion Foundation, her organization weighs in with about 5,500 members. And a spokesperson for the American Humanist Association put its membership at 7,300.

Without a doubt, the work of organizations such as the Freedom from Religion Foundation, which works tirelessly to maintain the separation of church and state, is essential to the protection of non-believers' rights. But given that three of the most renowned Freethought organizations in America are largely reliant on the revenue garnered from fewer than 20,000 annual memberships, the need to form broader alliances is irrefutable. While Ellen Johnson

---

9. Jeff Nall. "2005 Survey of Belief and Support for the Separation of Church and State" (June 2005). In total I polled 28 liberals, who responded to an email survey. 8 respondents were Christian, 6 were religious but not Christian ("Others"), 7 were either Atheists or Agnostics, and 7 identified with no particular religion, but were inclined to a belief in the supernatural.
10. Jeff Nall. "2005 Survey of Belief and Support for the Separation of Church and State" (June 2005).
11. Ibid.

contends that atheists *are* "joiners," but prefer to join at a local level,[12] the effectiveness of independent local groups in taking on important issues like the protection of the separation of church and state is questionable, and very difficult to accurately gage: how many of the forty-seven local atheists groups, listed on AA's website, have a purely social function? How many generate revenue, and how much? How many make legal challenges over church and state issues? How many have a well-crafted plan of action? Moreover, if the bulk of atheists are joining at a local level, rather than through national groups, why are multi-chapter state groups like the Atheists of Florida so small? According to a spokesperson for the group, which has chapters in Miami/Ft. Lauderdale, Tampa Bay, Sarasota, and a business headquarters in Ft. Pierce, Atheists of Florida has between 150 to 175 members, as of June 2005.

Even if local community groups were successful in attracting more Freethinkers than the national organizations, there is only so much they can do without the direct support of centralized, formally functioning organizations, equipped with qualified leaders, lawyers, strategies, and substantial financial resources. To fully put this matter into perspective, we must take a quick glance at our opposition, the Religious Right: Consider that the political arm of the radical group, Focus on the Family, "raised nearly $9 million in its first six months of existence."[13] But that is just a primer. The Family Research Council (www.Frc.org) has over 400,000 members and generates about $10 million each year; the Alliance Defense Fund, the ACLU of the radical right, earns nearly $18 million each year; the Christian Coalition of America (www.cc.org) has at least 300,000 members, and earned more than $4 million in 2001; Jerry Falwell

---

12. Ellen Johnson, phone interview by author, 20 June 2005. "The old things that atheists are not joiners," said Johnson, "they are joiners, they are joiners. They're joining local groups, they're just not joining the national groups."

13. *Associated Press*, "Millions pour in for Focus on the Family's political offshoot," 3 June 2005, # HYPERLINK "http://www.summitdaily.com/article/20050603/NEWS/50603022/0/FRONTPAGE"# HYPERLINK "http://www.summitdaily.com/article/20050603/NEWS/50603022/0/FRONTPAGE"www.summitdaily.com/article/20050603/NEWS/50603022/0/FRONTPAGE (accessed 28 June 2005). For a detailed comparison between the size and wealth of Freethought organizations and the Religious Right, see appendix 4.

Ministries brought in more than $15 million in 2003; and Focus on the Family makes about $136 million a year, which it puts to use in reaching "2.3 million subscribers to their ten monthly magazines."[14] Comparatively, AA, FFRF, the Institute for Humanist Studies, the Council for Secular Humanism, and the Center for Inquiry collectively earned less than $8 million in 2003. As it now stands, the Freethought movement is a flea on the sleeve of the Religious Right. If non-believers truly desire to stand up against the maniacal beast of religious zealotry, they must accept the very basic and well-founded conclusion that true atheists are in short supply, and those willing to contribute to national organizations are scarcer.

To overcome the disadvantages of being vastly outnumbered, and horribly under-funded, Freethinkers must turn to religious allies. Whereas true atheists account for about 2 percent of the United States population, those who identify with a religion other than Christianity account for somewhere between 3.7 percent and 8.4 percent. While 2001 ARIS reports that only 3.7 percent of the population are non-Christian religionists, a 2002 report by the National Opinion Research Center (NORC) at the University of Chicago, estimates that number to be much higher: 8.4 percent (6.9 "Other" and 1.5 "Jewish"). Not only are there more non-Christian religionists than there are atheists, according to NORC's 2002 General Social Survey, the "others" are the fastest growing group in America. Based on the report's monitoring of the United States' religious belief, the number of "other" religionists (excluding Jews) has increased by about 360 percent over three decades. Meanwhile, "nones" have grown by about 270 percent. Since many in the minority religious community share non-believers' abhorrence of efforts by Christian extremists to erect a theocracy in the United States, Freethinkers should work diligently to befriend this growing segment of the population.

Like Freethinkers, almost every non-Christian religious group has a clearly delineated interest in maintaining the separation of

---

14. For details on these groups and dozens more that comprise the Radical Right, go to www.pfaw.org/pfaw/general/default.aspx?oid=3796. Info on annual revenue can also be obtained through www.guidestar.org.

church and state. Take for instance the intolerance experienced by Jews at the U.S. Air Force Academy. In May 2005, Jews complained that the academy had created an unfriendly environment for non-Protestant Christians. Apparently the Academy had officially sponsored Christian programs, including the showing of Mel Gibson's film Passion of the Christ, and an Academy chaplain even "directed the cadets in attendance to proselytize those who did not attend. The penalty for those who failed to accept the proselytizing was to 'burn in the fires of hell.'"

Among the minority religions, Wicca, the fastest growing religion in the nation, percentage-wise, is one of the most reviled by religious extremists. In April 2005, a "panel of the Fourth Circuit Court of Appeals in Virginia ruled" "that the Chesterfield County Board of Supervisors could" prohibit a Wiccan spiritual leader from delivering a religious invocation at their board meetings. In May 2005, a judge in Indiana issued an order prohibiting two divorced Wiccan parents from exposing their nine-year-old boy to "non-mainstream religious beliefs and rituals." Non-Christian religionists continue to be increasingly targeted by religious fanatics. Clearly these groups share non-believers' concerns about the advancement of religion in the public, secular sphere.

Not only are minority religionists equally interested in preserving a purely secular government, many are already ardent separation of church and state activists. In May 2005, Zen-Buddhist David Musgrove took on Florida's Brevard County Public School Board when the principal of his daughter's school, Palm Bay High, chose a Calvary Chapel church as the location for the school's graduation. Proving that atheists and minority religionist alliances can work, Musgrove teamed up with atheist parent, Dianna Narciso in taking the school to Federal court over the church setting. Though the lateness of the call to stop the graduation forced Federal District Judge Gregory A. Presnell to allow the ceremonies to be held, the judge made it clear he thought the proceedings were unconstitutional. He said officials should have chosen a different facility not only out of deference to everyone, including non-Christians, but also "to maintain the separation of church and state that has allowed religion in this country to flourish." He also said, "I don't necessarily approve of the school board's decision because it seems clear to me that a secular facility without these religious icons should have been chosen." Five months later, in October 2005, the school board voted unanimously to end the battle, barring itself "from holding graduation ceremonies for any schools in Brevard County School District in churches or any other houses of worship in which religious iconography is visible to participants or to anyone in attendance on either the outside or the inside of the building."

We have a Buddhist and atheist alliance to laud for this outcome.

Many atheists may be surprised to learn just how often our concerns about infringements of the separation of church and state are shared by religious leaders. Though the local media did not represent such views, in speaking to various religious leaders throughout Central Florida, I discovered that many were equally appalled by the Brevard County School Board's selection of a church for graduation. Cantor Pat Hickman of the Temple Israel, in Viera Florida said:

> I think most of the people in my community were uncomfortable with the idea of having a public school graduation in a facility that had very strong symbols of one particular faith. I think that there are lots of other places that public schools can have their ceremonies, where they don't exclude anybody or make anybody feel uncomfortable even if there are just a few people in the graduating class who are another faith. It didn't seem appropriate to me.

Cantor Hickman also said she cherishes the separation of church and state as a definitive feature of our nation:

> I feel that it's very important to keep the separation of church and state. That our country was founded giving the greatest blessing of religious freedom. It was founded by people who were escaping religious persecution. I think our founding fathers were very smart in giving those kinds of blessings to all people. And I think that as soon as you start getting religion too mixed into politics and government that there's a danger in that.

Swamiji Chid Ghan Anand, Spiritual Leader of the Shri Shiv Dham Hindu Temple in Orlando, Florida, agreed: "As long as this is a democratic country, and as long as there is freedom of expression... it should not be forced in the law books that you do something for Christians because it is for Christians, because you don't consider what will happen with non-Christians."

On the subject of the graduation, Swamiji said a religiously neutral site should always be selected. "(The venue) should not be related to a religion because there are many people going to that school who are not Christian or maybe not related to Christians or maybe don't want to be related to Christians."

Reflecting on the bigger picture, Rev. Ann Fuller, a Unitarian Universalist, said she feels particularly threatened by activist judges who show no regard for the separation of church and state:

> There are times I feel like I'm already living in a theocracy. One of my greatest fears is seeing the stories that come through about judgments from the bench that are made based on religion rather than law. For example, the situation in Indiana. That's just something beyond the pale. It's threatening enough to me that congress would pass laws and the Executive branch would suggest laws that infringe upon our religious rights, but the fact that judges are already making religious decisions without any law that supports them, I find incredibly alarming.

Reverence for the separation of church and state, however, does not simply start with atheists and end with non-Christians. A rising number of Christians believe churches are too directly involved in politics, and that our nation benefits from a firm separation of church and state. Rev. Alicia S. Rapp, of the Florida based Palm Bay Riviera United Church of Christ, said her church works hard to keep God and government separate:

> We don't allow the voter (booths). So we don't tell our folks who to vote for. ...we don't allow politics to cross over into our congregation.... When I preach from the pulpit I also preach about the war and those kinds of things. ...but I don't say if you vote for George Bush or one way or another. And that's the separation of church and state issue.

Rev. Rapp also takes issue with churches that use the guise of benevolence to gain entry into the public sphere, only to propagandize their organization's ideology:

> Our church is right next door to an elementary school. We specifically chose this piece of property to be next door to a public school, because we don't build private schools. We believe in helping in the public schools. ... We send mentors over there and we buy school supplies for the school, we do all kinds of things, but we don't tuck notes in there, saying who it's from. We don't proselytize.

Rev. Rapp went on to explain how, just a few days after the contended Florida high school graduation took place at a church, she was frustrated to find the boundaries of separation of church and state garishly blurred before her very eyes. Not only was her son's sixth grade public school graduation held at a Presbyterian church, after the ceremony members of the church enticed children with free tootsie-roll pops, and proceeded to give them flyers regarding the church's basketball camp and its vacation Bible school. When Rev. Rapp reached her car, she found yet another piece of church literature on her windshield: "And I know that the church was just thinking, 'hey this is a great time to market our church.' But I think of it as crossing the line."

While the United States is incontestably filled of religious zealots who wish to draw the mind's shades closed to reason and Constitutional values, atheists cannot afford to ignore the profusion of religionists who share our concerns. When atheists give credence to radical Christian claims that "all" Christians are this way or that way, we aid the promulgation of their illusion. Christian churches like the United Church of Christ (UCC), which became the largest Christian denomination to officially endorse same-sex marriage in July 2005, comprise a substantial portion of the Christians who populate our nation. According to the 2001 ARIS, not only are there more than 1,378,000 UCC Christians in the United States, .7 percent of the population, UCC numbers are on the rise. In the eleven years between 1990 and 2001, the churches numbers rose by about 230 percent, making it the thirteenth largest Christian denomination out of thirty-five. To date, there are about 5,700 UCC congregations in the United States.

Though many atheists may believe that pro-science, separation minded Christians are an infinitesimal minority, history shows otherwise. Christians like Rev. Martin Luther King openly supported the separation of church and state. In a 1965 interview with *Playboy*, King offered firm support for the U.S. Supreme Court's decision ruling school prayer unconstitutional:

> I endorse it. I think it was correct. Contrary to what many have said, it sought to outlaw neither prayer nor belief in God. In a pluralistic society such as ours, who is to determine what prayer shall be spoken, and by whom? Legally, constitutionally, or otherwise, the state certainly has no such right. I am strongly opposed to the efforts that have been made to nullify the decision.

King felt that it was to Christianity's advantage to be disjoined from the state. He said that the church "is not the master or the servant of the state, but rather the conscience of the state. It must be the guide and the critic of the state, and never its tool."

Proving that the opinions held by Rev. Rapp and Rev. King are no anomaly, The Christian Alliance for Progress (CAP), a newly formed Jacksonville-based organization, recently stated unequivocal support for the separation of church and state. Agreeing with King that the Christian church must be the critic and not the tool of the state, CAP stated the following, in a declaration aimed specifically at the Religious Right:

> We also reaffirm a well-established American commitment to a clear separation of church and state. In your statements you often characterize America as a "Christian nation." We strongly disagree. As a nation of immigrants, America has been a land of freedom and diversity. Separation of church and state helps ensure liberty and justice for all Americans - not just those who are like-minded.

Beyond supporting the separation of church and state, CAP's spokesman, Rev. Timothy F. Simpson has directly stated his willingness to work with atheists: "An atheist who stands for the interests of the neighbor, an atheist who stands for the interests of poor people at the margins, for the oppressed, is worth more than a hundred Christians who have made their bed with the fat cats, because that atheist is actually articulating the ends of the kingdom of God."

While Ellen Johnson asserts that religion "has been the driving force behind...the opposition to...state-church separation," the dual-reality is that believers are also the driving force to keep church and state separate. According to Rob Boston, Assistant Director of Communications for Americans United, the many religious voices that do speak out for the separation of church and state are invaluable to the cause.

> ...I do believe it is important for non-believers to acknowledge that many religious people support and defend the separation of church and state - and that those folks add a powerful and needed voice to this issue. For example, in Washington, the Baptist Joint Committee for Religious Liberty strongly supports church-state separation, arguing that the wall of separation is the best vehicle to defend freedom of conscience for all. Over the years, Americans United has worked with Methodists, Lutherans, Jews, Presbyterians, Unitarians, Quakers, Seventh day Adventists and many others. I have seen these groups defend the rights of non-believers just as they would the rights of a Christian. We must all work together and not let issues of theology divide us. A failure to stay united only helps the Religious Right.

Rather than making an enemy of the whole of religion, non-believers should make friends of those who are moderate and share their appreciation for the sanctity of the Constitution and its wall between church and state. Once this is done, atheists might then concentrate on strengthening organizations like Americans United. While standing strong at 75,000 members as of June 2005, the U.S.'s best church and state watch dog is without a local presence in nearly 20 states. In total, there are just 58 local chapters across the nation, 34 of which are located in just seven states. Atheists could profoundly impact the struggle to keep church and state separate by forging alliances with local religious leaders and erecting local chapters of Americans United around the country, especially in states with few to no chapters. Another organization Freethinkers might work with is The Interfaith Alliance (TIA). While Americans United concentrates specifically on dealing with infringements on the separation of church and state, TIA focuses on building grass-roots alliances between people of all faiths and no faith—the group specifically mentions atheists and agnostics. With a purported 150,000 members, TIA offers Freethinkers a unique opportunity to work with people of a variety of faiths to ensure the rights of all, including those of non-belief, are not only accepted but also protected. The organization also serves the important purpose of highlighting the U.S.'s prospering pluralism, which directly undermines the contentions and the agenda of the Religious Right. (TIA even allots small grants to several new local groups each year.)

One of the salient obstacles hindering Freethinkers from forging common-sense alliances with rational, free-thinking religionists is the common tendency of non-believers to espouse indiscriminate contempt and condescension for people of faith. Tossing aside mutual respect, many atheist writers even openly advocate the intolerant and insipid strategy of ridiculing others' beliefs. In the preface of his book, *Atheism: A Reader*, editor S.T. Joshi writes: "Even ridicule of religion is an entirely valid enterprise." Joshi is not alone in this opinion. In an article on the AA website, Eddie Tabash defends the right to "bash" other religions: "Establishing the social acceptability of *ridiculing* (emphasis mine) the absurdities of religious claims is an integral part of gaining acceptance for secular humanism." And the Atheists of Florida have among their stated purposes this derogatory gem: "To promote the concept that believers of any faith, are the *deluded* (emphasis mine) victims of unfounded dogmas toward whom sympathy and under-standing should be extended." As if those examples were not enough to give atheism a bad name, the comments of Dr. Timothy Shortell, which recently came to light, are much more divisive. When Shortell was elected to the position of chair of the department of sociology at Brooklyn College, Jim Brown, a reporter for the Christian news service, *Agape Press*, reported Shortell's having once described religious people as "an ugly, violent lot" and "moral retards." Brown also quotes Shortell as having written that "Christians claim theirs is a faith based on love, but they'll just as soon kill you." The quotes are from a piece Shortell published online, entitled "Religion & Morality: A Contradiction Explained." In the piece Shortell lambastes religion, and levies wild, erratic generalizations which succeed in little more than feeding into the Religious Right's Christian persecution propaganda:

> On a personal level, religiosity is merely annoying—like bad taste. This immaturity represents a significant social problem, however, because religious adherents fail to recognize their limitations. So, in the name of their faith, these moral retards are running around pointing fingers and doing real harm to others. One only has to read the newspaper to see the results of their handiwork. They discriminate, exclude and belittle. They make a virtue of closed-mindedness and virulent ignorance. They are an ugly, violent lot.

Some Freethinkers, however, sharply reproach the such use of ridicule, as well as the unfounded generalizations that excite such derision. Dylan Evans, an atheist and academic from the United Kingdom, writes: "the kind of atheism that flourishes today is old and tired." He goes on to write that "[n]ot believing in God is no excuse for being virulently anti-religious or naively pro-science." Torben Riise, a veteran Humanist speaker and writer on science and ethics, says that when Freethinkers levy rancorous diatribes against another person's belief system, they end up emulating the very fundamentalists they loathe. Riise writes that he has "at numerous occasions noted that Humanists refer to and characterize our 'opponents' in the same stereotyping and belittling ways that we resent and blame others for using about Humanists." While Riise acknowledges "the value of polarization," he nonetheless concludes that such "is a strategy, which draws fire and escalates a spiral of negativism in which no one wins."

Jennifer Hancock, Executive Director for the Humanists of Florida Association (HFA), says the use of ridicule is not only ineffective, it is often based on erroneous generalizations that are an affront to reason and common sense.

> I think (ridicule) is offensive. It is a form of religious bigotry. When I

hear someone say Catholics are stupid, they are talking about people I love and care about, who are definitely not stupid. Plus, if it
happens to someone's face, exactly how are you going to have a
good conversation with someone you just told was stupid. I am an
atheist, but that is my personal belief. I don't understand why people believe, and truth be told, belief doesn't make sense to me. But I
know from my friends and family members that as wacky as their
belief is to me, my unbelief is just as wacky to them. So, the key is to
accept that people really do believe what they say they do, and this
is a matter of basic respect (until or unless the person you are talking to becomes rude, which sometimes, but not often, happens).

The simplistic generalizations, made by some Freethinkers, tend
to reflect ignorance about the diversity of beliefs and opinions held by
the very diverse population of believers in the United States. While
many of the generalizations made by religion-bashing atheists are
sometimes true, American religious belief is so varied that nothing
short of needle-point accuracy and specificity will suffice. Sadly, many
Freethinkers are so often looking to discredit religion as a whole, that
they frequently include myriad liberal, science-minded religionists in
their sweeping assaults. To write, as Shortell has, that "religious adherents" "discriminate, exclude and belittle," as well as "make a virtue of closed-mindedness and virulent ignorance" is to indiscriminately bomb a metropolis filled with diverse religious traditions and
beliefs, when the scorching bombardment was meant for but a small
warehouse of radical religious fanaticism. *New Republic* writer, and
self-described "non-believer," Alan Wolfe, hammers this point home
when he writes: "non-believers have long been known for the shrillness of their tone, their thinly disguised contempt for people they can
barely understand, and their conviction (you might even call it religious) that they always have been and always will be on the right side
of history." Wolfe goes on to ask whether these militant advocates of
atheism "will recognize how much belief has changed since the days
of the Enlightenment, let alone over the past half-century in America,
and how much non-belief has to change to keep up."

One of the more popular assumptions made by many Freethinkers is that religious belief almost always results in antipathy to ra-

tionalism and science; as if to suggest only atheists can properly respect science and reason. In reality, nothing could be further from the truth. For example, explained Jennifer Hancock, "I dated a devote Lutheran once. He was a great scientist." According to Swamiji Chid Ghan Anand, his religion's revered text, the Vedas "says the more science will develop, the more the religion will open itself;" and that science "is a part" of his religion. Interestingly, Swamiji, who represents a religious body that has tripled in just eleven years here in the U.S., went on to articulate a seemingly atheist view, that human beings who rely on faith alone are lost:

> The thing is now, human beings, now especially, who are based on faith only, they are lost. Just mark my words, they are lost. ... They are looking for answers (but) according to logic, you can not find those answers in a belief system. In a belief system you have only to accept, and that's it. Whatever is told to you accept otherwise you are not a part of the community, or you are maybe a sinner. You can not question something, while in science everything is questioned.

Other religious leaders like Cantor Hickman expressed an equal respect for science. Explaining her ability to reconcile her religious beliefs and the discoveries of modern science, Cantor Hickman said: "I think there's a lot of spirituality in modern science." Adding, "I think you just have to be open to it. I don't feel really in conflict. I really don't."

According to Zen-Buddhist teacher and writer Al Rapaport, who produced a series of conferences on Buddhism across the U.S a few years ago: "The Zen viewpoint doesn't have any conflict with modern science, and indeed modern science has confirmed views of time and space that have been taught in Buddhism for thousands of years." Proving that atheists are not the only ones whose beliefs are rooted in scientific thought, Rapaport went on to explain, "Evolution is a fact. Everything is in a process of evolving all the time. This again is Buddhist teaching."

In my own research, in which I surveyed a group of socio-political liberals, I found that religion did not play a key factor in determining their opinions regarding church-state separation and the value of science. Seven of the eight liberal Christians I surveyed affirmed that their religious viewpoints do *not* conflict with the discoveries of modern science. One Christian even noted: "On the contrary, the first chapter of Genesis' account of creation is similar to Darwin's theory." And all six "Other," non-Christian religionists, that I surveyed came to the same conclusion. One respondent, who practices "Native American" religion, said, "we have not propped up our core beliefs on dogma. We are encouraged to learn and grow. Truth is what it is, not what we wish to make it." Another respondent, a self-described Pagan, said the following when asked if he/she believed in evolution: "Do I believe in gravity, or the Theory of Relativity? It's not a matter of belief, it's a matter of fact." Clearly, many religionists prize science in the same way atheists do. (Based on these findings, one might even theorize that political outlooks can shape perspectives on the separation of church and state, and science as much as religious belief.) In fact, near the height of the 2005 "intelligent design" debate, CAP succeeded in debunking a bundle of stereotypes when it denounced "intelligent design" as pseudoscience and stated its unequivocal support for real science: "Evolution is widely accepted as incontrovertible in science communities *and faith communities* across the world."

Overall, this issue highlights the before mentioned problem articulated by Alan Wolfe: when will atheists "recognize how much belief has changed since the days of the Enlightenment, let alone over the past half-century in America...." Regardless of how Freethinkers view such marriages, many religionists have found ways to comfortably synthesize their religious beliefs with a profound respect for science and reason. So if anti-science and anti-reason, anti-humanity fundamentalists are the true target of Freethinkers, why bombard rational religionists with rancorous attacks? The solution, clearly, is to recognize that all religions are not the same; nor are all religious denominations of a specific religion made the same. The fact is, religionists who value science and reason share an equal interest, with atheists, in stopping fundamentalists from subverting centuries of progress. The last thing Freethinkers should do is to offend science and reason loving religionists.

The Freethought community's identification with the negation of belief, and, as a result, its association with antipathy is equally problematic. According to author Alister McGrath, also a professor of historical theology at Oxford University: "atheism spawns organizations; it does not create community... the community thus created seems to be based solely on distaste for religion." While atheists have long sought to dispel such a notion, there is a wealth of evidence to support at least a partial acknowledgement of such criticism. Consider, for instance, the testimony given by a leader in the Freethought community who asked not to be identified:

> Our biggest problem in the Humanist movement... is keeping atheists who just want to complain about people of faith, out of our organization. .... They join then get upset that we aren't focused on bashing religion, but we have to tell them that that isn't our mission, and perhaps they should join a group whose sole purpose is to bash religion.

That so many indolent bashers exist within the Freethought community is hardly surprising considering the popularity of shirts that feature such slogans as: "I (heart) Roman Lions," "Christ on Boards" (image of Christ nailed to cross), "We Won, Jesus Died," and "I (image of Roman Lion) Xtians"; not to mention the kinds of jokes one finds on atheist websites. According to Alister McGrath, Great Britain's atheist network, National Secular Society once posted this one: "What's the difference between Jesus and a painting? It only takes one nail to hang a painting."

Ironically, the concentration on ridiculing faith and evangelizing atheism is not only making it difficult to befriend the faithful, it is creating an indolent arm-chair atheism that is more concerned with argumentation than setting and accomplishing goals. At bottom, atheists are faced with a question: do you want to spend your time and resources trying to convert people to atheism, or will your agenda be defending the freedom of disbelief, which, as Jennifer Hancock put it, "is a completely different thing." Those favoring proselytizing in the name of atheism are in need of a serious awakening. The idyllic hope that Freethought will miraculously spread across the globe like a vaccine, *saving* humanity from the pestilence of religion, has all the characteristics of a wild fantasy. Religion will likely flourish as it has since time immemorial, until the end of civilization. As it stands, the vast majority of Americans, 84 percent, say that religion is important in their life. By bashing religion, we polarize ourselves from a plethora of free-thinking religious persons, and relegate American atheism to the shadows of an unpleasant fanaticism. As Unitarian Universalist Rev. Ann Fuller explained:

> Whether you're an atheist or a theist, you have to admit that ultimately, you don't really know for sure, for somebody else. You may know for yourself, which is really a belief, but you can not know what the right belief path for anyone else.…
>
> To expect everyone to believe and think the same way is preposterous.

In order to defend the separation of church and state, we must, as Rob Boston of Americans United puts it, respect the beliefs of others:

> Many of our members are religious believers, but a significant number are non-religious. We welcome everyone to this cause, but all of our allies must be willing to work alongside one another in an atmosphere of cooperation and mutual respect. There is no place for religion bashing at Americans United.

Each day, Christian extremists move closer to transforming the United States into the Christian nation they pretend it always has been. With major funding and countless backers, the Religious Right has made great strides in its efforts to take over our the three branches of our government, rewrite history, and debunk truth and reason, forever. As it stands, the Freethought community is unable to mount a sufficient defense against this torrential assault: our movement is too small, too unpopular, too under-financed, and, in some cases, too dogmatic in its antipathy toward religious people.

To face these challenges, the Freethought movement, like all movements, must evolve. Religion in the United States can not be vilified or even typified by the generalizations of the 19th and 20th century. Today's Christianity is hardly the largely monolithic ideology it once was: many Christians challenge traditional interpretations of scripture, including literal understandings of the Bible's message; many are opening their doors to gays and lesbians; some argue in support of evolution. Unlike decades past, many Americans are choosing rather than inheriting their religion: as a result non-traditional religions are growing exponentially. The very dynamic of religion, the purpose and meaning of religion is being reconsidered, and, in some ways reinvented. More than ever, 21st century atheists need to turn to the founding fathers, many of whom believed in a Supreme Being, and continue the founders' vigilant criticism of religious *fanaticism*, rather than deriding all religion. Atheists can no longer afford to hold onto the fantasy that humankind will one day see religion through the lens of atheism. As Voltaire once wrote, "It would be the height of folly to pretend to bring all men to have the same thoughts in metaphysics. It would be easier to subdue the whole universe by arms than to subdue all the minds in a single city." Instead, non-believers must hone their criticisms to suit the times and, rather than attacking religion as a whole, they must target the kind of *radical* religiosity enlightened minds like Voltaire and Spinoza disdained: the kind that spews intolerance, hatred, and dogmatic conformity from the pulpit.

To realize this objective, Freethinkers must first befriend those whose backs, like their own, are firmly pressed to the wall separating church and state, as if they would willingly sacrifice their lives for the First Amendment. Individually, such groups are small, disregarded minorities: atheists, humanists, agnostics; liberal Christians, Unitarians, Buddhists, Jews, Hindus; Wiccans, pagans, Native Americans. But collectively, these groups are the "Others," a powerful, swelling chorus, equally reverent of the words: "Congress shall make no law respecting an establishment of religion...." By forging alliances with church and state separationists, removing faith-stereotypes from discourse, Freethinkers can improve their image around the nation, and show that they do have a sense of community beyond the world of antipathy.

Above all else, Freethinkers *must* realize that their legal right to disbelieve is, ironically, largely reliant on the support of open-minded religionists. To protect their rights, non-believers must befriend the free-thinking faithful. In doing so, they will make impenetrable, the wall defending their right to reject that which they do not believe in.

—Originally published in Volume 14 (2006) of the journal,
Essays in the Philosophy of Humanism.

A New Progressive Alliance:

A Call for Unity Between Secular, Spiritual,

and Religious Progressives

⋈

Since the start of the Iraq war, the surge in American-based religious fanaticism, and the birth of both my daughter and my activist spirit, I've become less interested in nourishing discord and firmly dedicated to discovering ethical commonality. Simply put, the destructive, inhumane, and theocratic impulses of our nation caused me to realize the need for greater unity among political progressives, regardless of their religious perspectives.

I began my part-time campaign in 2004 when I wrote an article entitled, "Turning to Friends in Faithful Places: Why Non-Theists Must Befriend Likeminded, Minority Religious Groups." As the title suggests the piece called for secular-Humanists/atheists to set aside their distaste for religion and unite with people of minority religious groups. My argument was that non-Christians, the "others," 1) shared secularists concerns over the collision of church and state and were just as concerned about the rise of Christian theocrats. And 2) that between those who do not affiliate with any particular religion (often referred to as "nones" and the "others" (non-Christians) were (and still are) on the statistical rise, and would, if not now, be a potent force in the near future.

I sent the article to the editor of a now defunct progressive bi-monthly magazine called *IMPACT press*. Shortly thereafter, I received an email from the main editor with the comments of the co-editor who had reviewed the article. He offered some quality mechanical suggestions and said he liked my use of statistics and the way I put the religion-in-America issue into perspective. But he rebuffed my central thesis, my purpose for writing the article, as "naïve." He dismissed my call for unity as "flawed." He wrote: "I find it unlikely that freethinkers and people of faith will join hands for any purpose for any length of time." He went on to suggest that I "find a different focal point, so it's not a total waste." I responded by telling the main editor that even *Reason* magazine had shown an interest in the piece in its original form—Reason ultimately decided against the piece because it didn't fit the theme of the issue they were working on—and urged him to reconsider publishing the piece.

After some mechanical revision, the article ran in the October/November 2004 issue of *IMPACT press*. "Turning to Friends in Faithful Places: Why Non-Theists Must Befriend Likeminded, Minority Religious Groups" was an immediate success. The idea of uniting such groups was widely praised and the article was posted or republished on numerous websites between the United States and Canada. It appeared on a range of websites belonging to a variety of groups, particularly Wiccan groups.

I continued this growing effort by participating in the 2005 Secular Student Alliance conference at Ohio State University where I presented a paper calling on secularists to unite with not only those in minority religions but also progressive Christians. Supporting the plausibility of a real alliance with people of varied beliefs, I specifically pointed to the efforts of a Buddhist and an atheist who had recently allied themselves to decry a violation of the separation of church and state in Brevard County, Florida, where I lived at the time. My presentation, in part, hinged on the wide support for their church-state separation activism among the half-dozen religious leaders I interviewed from around Central Florida.

Encouraged by conversations with prominent Humanists like former Florida Humanist Association director, Jennifer Hancock, and UK atheist Dylan Evans' article, "The 21st century atheist: Not believing in God is no excuse for being virulently anti-religious or naively pro-science" (*The Guardian* 5/2/2005), I called on secularists to renounce antagonism and to turn their attention to the zealots seeking to corrupt the constitution. A few months later, in October, I joined the Association for Humanist Sociology's 30th annual meeting where I pointed to Martin Luther King as a clear example of the shared values of secular and religious progressives. I specifically talked about King's focus on the wellbeing of people in the here and now, his disdain for the corruption of organized religion, and his absolute support of the separation of church and state. Though relatively seldom mentioned by the right, King told Playboy magazine that he fully agreed with the Supreme Court's decision to take government mandated prayer out of public schools.

In May 2006, after conducting several inspiring interviews with key progressive Christian leaders and researching organizations on the religious left, I gave a lecture at the American Humanists Association's (AHA) annual conference. The talk, *Why Humanists Should and Must Befriend the Progressive Faithful,* introduced the secular-Humanist audience to a handful of progressive Christian leaders including Rev. Tim Simpson of the Christian Alliance for Progress and James R. Adams, founder of The Center for Progressive Christianity. I insisted that only by allying with such organizations, could secularists defeat the religious and radical right and revive our progressive vision of the United States. I was thrilled when the majority in the audience responded approvingly. Not long after, my article (published in this collection) "Overcoming Antagonistic Atheism to Recast the Image of Humanism" was published in *The Humanist* and became well-circulated. The piece has spurned debate about the way in which the secular-Humanist movement should engage believers.

Finally, in the early part of 2006 these efforts culminated in a statement *against* antagonism and *for* unity between secular, spiritual, and religious progressives. A draft was circulated among about one-dozen people, both secular and religious, who reviewed, commented on, offered suggestions, and in some way or another contributed to the manifesto. The two main co-authors besides me include Jennifer Hancock, mentioned earlier, and Humanist Chaplain of Harvard University, Greg M. Epstein. What follows is the text of this call for unity.

A New Progressive Alliance:
A Call for Unity between Secular, Spiritual, and Religious Progressives

Realizing that our shared commitment to human rights, religious freedom, and peace and social justice, significantly outweighs our differences; we the undersigned, comprised of both secular and religious progressives, declare an alliance between progressive, rational-minded people regardless of one's spiritual, religious, or secular perspective.

While our beliefs about the existence of God may differ, progressive Americans share a common tradition of humanism dating back to at least the Renaissance. Many spiritual and religious thinkers have significantly contributed to the advancement of doubt, free thinking, and the sciences, laying the ground work for the Enlightenment and modernity. There is no "cultural war" dividing us.

While we make no apologies for the beliefs that have helped to shape our character, we acknowledge that neither faith in God nor atheism suffices to define one's ethical character. We maintain that the character of a human being can only be defined and evaluated on the basis of one's actions.

We agree that fanaticism, be it religious or secular, is the true enemy of reason and of human progress.

We therefore formally reject the proposition that one cannot be both religious and rational. And we patently reject the notion that people of faith are incapable of respecting modern science and evolution.

We equally reject the point of view that implies one must believe in God or hold a specific religious belief in order to be valued as a moral/ethical being.

We call upon our movements to unite for the betterment of our society and to reject the enmity of pundits who have made their careers out of promoting intolerance and hatred.

We affirm the plurality of our nation and the importance of maintaining the wall of separation between civic and religious authorities in order to preserve the democratic principle of freedom of and from religion.

Our nation has been carved into a maze of horrors: torture, war, poverty, gross spending on warfare, corruption, religious fanaticism, sexism, homophobia, bigotry and intolerance. Progressive people both with and without religious faith must work together if we are to correct these injustices.

We, the undersigned, agree that given our nation's many ethical and societal challenges, secular, spiritual and religious progressives must set aside their differences to work together to create a better world.

June 3, 2006

A clear rejection of the simplistic dichotomy of 'atheists versus Christians,' as of early 2008 the small but impressive list of signatories include:

James Rowe Adams, Founder The Center for Progressive Christianity
Bill Broderick, Humanist, Atheist, proud Canadian and member of
    Humanist Association of Canada
Edd Doerr, immediate past president, American Humanist Association; president of Americans for Religious Liberty; Unitarian
    Universalist
Tom Ferrick, Humanist Association of Massachusetts.
Rev. Ann Fuller, Ministerial Intern, Unitarian Universalist Church
    of Brevard

Rev. Fallon Glenn, Vice President and South Eastern Regional Director of the Pagan Unity Campaign and Public Relations Specialist for Pagans United www.pagansunited.com

Alice Kahn Ladas, Ed.D. Humanist Celebrant, AHA and NY Society for Ethical Culture

Hamish Macpherson, organizer of the O Project, championing atheists' contributions to society and promoting good relations with all faiths

David Musgrove, Zen Buddhist, victorious plaintiff in Musgrove vs. Brevard School Board church-state case

Michele Paccione, Christian Peace Activist

Rev. Jim Rigby, Pastor of St. Andrew's Presbyterian Church in Austin, TX, and longtime Activist

Stephen Rockwell, Managing Director and co-founder of CrossLeft

Rev. Timothy F. Simpson, Interim President of the Christian Alliance for Progress; minister in the Presbyterian Church USA

Robert Stephens, Ph.D., Founder and current President of Darwin Day celebration, http://www.darwinday.org/

Dr. Michael Stepniak, member of the American Humanist Association and Associate Dean of Performing Arts at Adelphi University

Laura M Wandrie, President/Founder, Pagans United

THE PASSION OF TOLERANCE:

RECLAIMING JESUS FOR

HUMAN PEACE AND JUSTICE

ⵣ

Tortured. Beaten bloody. Humiliated. All before enemies and friends alike. Denied freedom, compassion, and dignity. Those are some of the many characteristics the innocent prisoners at the U.S. manned Abu Ghraib prison in Iraq shared with Jesus Christ. The vile photos and details of Abu Ghraib repulsed the world when they were first released in 2004, revealing that some detainees were "ridden like animals, fondled by female soldiers, forced to curse their religion and required to retrieve their food from toilets" [1] — unsettling reminders of the kind of horrific malevolence that led Jesus to the cross and still exists in our world today. Such indifference for humanity and disdain for human life also beckons us to re-evaluate the scope of the biblical account of Jesus' crucifixion, specifically through Mel Gibson's film, *The Passion of the Christ,* in the hopes of better understanding the motives of intolerance and hatred. What promotes, in humankind, such timeless savagery? Are we prompted by ignorance, prejudice and fear, or is it simply a desire

---

1. "Report: Soldiers Fondled Iraqi Prisoners," *Associated Press.*

for power and dominion over others that subjects our ethics to disregard? And why has the iconoclastic, humanistic Jesus, the symbol of revolution that inspired Martin Luther King to wage war on injustice, become the tool of the unjust?

At the time of its highly anticipated release, in 2004, Mel Gibson's film roused worshipers' feelings of sympathy, gratefulness, and painful guilt. Very little, however, was said about the film's broader resonance—the indictment of intolerance and hate, and their product: torture and abuse. On the film's opening day, news programs questioned people exiting theaters; most remarked that the film helped them better understand the torment Jesus endured in order to die for their sins. Lori Rose, from Buffalo New York, told National Public Radio (NPR), "Anybody that believes in the story of the crucifixion of Jesus is going to be very emotional watching it." Rev. Travis Pittock, a Lutheran missionary, said, "Each time I've seen the movie my faith grows and grows and grows." Others outside of the Christian faith appreciated the work's potency, yet seemed preoccupied with disowning the work's divine nature. After seeing the film on opening night, moviegoer Carolyn Boday told NPR: "It's a great work of fiction, is what it is." Like most viewers, Father Vincent Higher, Director of Office for the Academic and Interreligious Affairs for Catholic Archdiocese was primarily concerned with the film's religious validity. "I think it's a tremendous dramatic portrayal," he told NPR, "but it's a piece of art. I didn't find it as faithful to the gospels as being touted."[2] In a letter to the editor, published in the April 2004 issue of *Freethought Today*, moviegoer Chris Benedict of Missouri wrote of the film: "The film actually plays around with the biblical text, adding details and dialogue that aren't even in the four gospels, but without addressing any of the theological implications of the story, like how can you kill someone who's supposedly a god?"

Sadly, the story's broader commentary on ethics and its humanistic appeal for tolerance and love seemed to have been ignored, partly because some non-Christians simply disdained the work as

---

2. "Audience Reaction to 'The Passion,'" *Natl. Public Radio* WFIT, Melbourne. 25, Feb. 2004. < http://www.npr.org/features/feature.php?wfId=1700786>.

merely a tool for proselytizing, while Christian patrons were so profoundly moved by Jesus' religiously motivated sacrifice, or disappointed with the film's inaccuracy, they found it almost impossible to extract a secular message from the film. But just as Thomas Jefferson and Benjamin Franklin were able to extract the secular virtue from Jesus' life, despite their having both expressed disbelief in his divinity and resurrection, so too can all Americans obtain the secular message of tolerance from The Passion. The very story of Christ and his crucifixion is laden with secular symbolism, representing temporal concerns. Throughout the gospels, Christ condemns wealth and the immoral life of luxury that follows; He instructs us against the counter productivity of violence that pits nation against nation, brother against brother. Even his own excruciating existence, from carpenter to sacrifice, represents all human suffering; he is an allusion to the plight endured by the world's under privileged or subjugated people.

Though many may see *The Passion of the Christ* as a strictly religious film, it simply is not. Unwittingly, Gibson has created a film that offers the most personal, candid, humanistic portrayal of Jesus, the living breathing man of flesh, ever. Who cannot recognize the universal truth which Jesus' pain and suffering convey, on screen, when Roman soldiers place the crown of thorns on his head, mock him, spit on him, beat him with the scepter, strip him and dress his body in the derogatory scarlet robe? (Mark 15:16-20). Is this kind of brutality so different from that which someone like Mathew Shepard, killed for his homosexuality, experienced? Shepard was robbed, pistol whipped more than a dozen times, humiliated, strung to a fence and left for dead. Initially mistaken for a scarecrow, he was found some 18 hours later, and eventually died in the hospital six days after being abducted. Ironically, it is Jesus' humanness, his mortality—the way his defenseless flesh is as easily torn from his body as that of Matthew Shepard—that evokes our sympathy, even empathy, sorrow, and horror; something a perfectly divine God, whose body is impervious to pain and bodily deterioration could not accomplish.

One does not need to be a Christian to be mortified by the 15 minutes of onscreen scourging that Jesus endures. New York Times writer, A. O. Scott was so repulsed by the film's violence he felt it was more successful at "assaulting the spirit" than it was in "uplifting it." Scott describes the intolerable violence in this way:

> Mr. Gibson has constructed an unnerving and painful spectacle that is also, in the end, a depressing one...the final hour of "The Passion of the Christ" essentially consists of a man being beaten, tortured and killed in graphic and lingering detail. Once he is taken into custody, Jesus (Jim Caviezel) is cuffed and kicked and then, much more systematically, flogged, first with stiff canes and then with leather whips tipped with sharp stones and glass shards. By the time the crown of thorns is pounded onto his head and the cross loaded onto his shoulders, he is all but unrecognizable, a mass of flayed and bloody flesh, barely able to stand, moaning and howling in pain.

For Scott, who echoes the opinions of many other film critics, the violence is simply too much to bear. So sanguinary is the movie, film critic Bob Mondello, in a review for NPR, said Gibson "has filmed what is quite possibly the bloodiest story every told." But in an age when wars are fought from computers like a video game—where human bodies are nothing more than blinking targets on a screen—there is something romantic and life affirming about a repulsion for brutality; it's like some long lost jewel, a forgotten virtue—humility, maybe even love. Setting it apart from common bloody action and horror films, *The Passion of The Christ* has the power to evoke humane sensitivity in a viewing audience accustom to rooting for righteous retribution.

The violence, however, should not merely repulse us, but also remind us of those persecuted people reflected in Jesus' agonizing face: millions of Jewish people at the hands of Hitler, millions of so-called witches burned, drowned, and tormented by the Church fathers during the misogynistic Witch Craze, as well as the brazen freethinkers like Giordano Bruno and so many more that suffered through the Inquisition. We can also see the agony of the African Americans slaves who had to hear, feel, and endure the brutal crack of the same persecutory whip.

In Jesus' face, we can see not just one person, but all people under the yoke of some oppressor. Having been both applauded and criticized for its excruciating detail, the film's morose depiction of Jesus' journey to the cross *is* painfully long. And it is in the mercilessness and monotony of Christ's death march that we are offered a glimpse at the cruel, impossible journey made by the Native American Cherokee tribe when President Andrew Jackson forced them to leave their land and take to the infamous Trail of Tears. Both were miserable, wretched treks, colored with human sacrifice.

According to renown scholar, John Crossan, the historical Jesus was actually preaching and acting against an oppressive system of classicism; and the Kingdom of God that he advocated was not something beyond this world, but "a community of radical or unbrokered equality in which individuals are in direct contact with one another and with God, unmediated by any established brokers or fixed locations."[3] Jesus was likely crucified, explains Crossan, as a result of his having upset authorities in Jerusalem with his radical "spiritual and economic egalitarianism."[4] Thus we should understand Jesus' crucifixion, as a sacrifice at the altar of a human fear, malice, and intolerance. Executed for railing against racism, crying out against mindless capitalism, Martin Luther King, too, was sacrificed at this very same altar, for the very same reasons. Again and again we find that the price of reform is justice sacrificed at the altar of malice, intolerance, fear, and hate. Without these willing and unwilling sacrifices, few of us would have the freedoms we know today.

Viewed in this light, Jesus' own struggle personifies those of people of all ages who have been brutalized and oppressed by an uncompromising and overwhelming majority: Pagans, Atheists, Muslims, unorthodox Christians, women, gays and lesbians, African Americans—everyone. All of these groups share the commonality of holding views contrary to that of the popular majority. Despite their innocence, the insatiable mob of all ages demands blood when their fears are aroused. Even when Pilate declares that he has "found no

---

3. John Dominic Crossan, *Jesus: A Revolutionary Biography* (New York: HarperCollins Publishers Inc., 1995.), 101.
4. Ibid., 133.

basis for your charges against [Jesus]" (Luke 23:14), the mob of Jesus' time, packed tightly into a comfortable frenzy of fear, shouts "crucify him" (Luke 23:20). Jesus' failure to conform earns him a death sentence. Justice is overrun by the frenzied rationalization that, because he does not respect the traditional values of the established religious authority, he is therefore a threat, and, being such, must be eliminated.

As is often the case, when ignorance and fear dominate conscience, once Jesus has been labeled a pariah, essentially demonized, the mob finds comfort, even acceptance in lashing out at him, blaming him for all of their misfortune. Yet, rather than simply finding the actions of those Jews and Romans responsible for Jesus' death appalling, through his horrific demise, the film provokes the question: how could these tormenters conquer their conscience in order to commit such crimes? After all, they were just men, with beating hearts, not monsters. This is, of course, the same question Americans must ask with regards to the crimes committed at Abu Ghraib, and similar crimes which, according to recent reports, have also been committed at Guantanamo Bay. *The Passion of the Christ* reveals the answer to both of these questions: humanity is eradicated in a process that begins with fear and ends in condoned hatred.

In these cases, soldiers went to extreme measures to torture their victim(s); in both cases, soldiers reportedly found revelry in the cruel spirit of their employment. But just as importantly, in both cases the soldiers carried out such criminal morbidity with the sanction of their leaders; despite Pilate's disclaimer—"I am innocent of the blood of this man. The responsibility is yours"—he *is* responsible for ordering the death of Jesus. Similarly, the loathsome acts occurring at Abu Ghraib resulted from consent of Defense Secretary, Donald Rumsfeld who "approved interrogation techniques that included "removal of clothing" and "inducing stress by use of detainee's fears (e.g. dogs.)"[5] Furthermore, neither the leaders nor the soldiers were solely responsible for the violence they perpetuated. Both groups were the instruments of the *people's* trepidation, which

---

5. John Diamond, "Rumsfeld Ok'd harsh treatment," *USA Today.* A1. Wednesday June 23, 2004.

permitted and even encouraged the Pharisees and Pilate to herd Jesus, no longer a human being among them, to his death. It was the people who forced Pilate to sentence Jesus to death. Even when Pilate gave the crowd a chance to choose Jesus, the pacifist, over Barabbas, the murder, they preferred the release of Barabbas; they chose barbarity, which was familiar, over the enlightened, peaceful teachings of Jesus, which were frighteningly new. Even those out-side of the frenzied mob, who sadly watched Jesus carry his cross, are complicit in his death, because they also resigned themselves to inaction. Likewise, our own fear, apathy and inaction, too, permitted the abuses at Abu Ghraib.

Ironically, the Jewish Pharisees of *The Passion of the Christ* bear a startling resemblance to the various Fundamentalist Christian lead-ers that have begun a campaign of hatred in the U.S. today. Just as Jesus was condemned by intolerant, religious leaders of his day, to-day men like Christian anti-gay rights activist, James Dobson, at-tempt to force their religious ideas on other Americans. Meanwhile politicians like George W. Bush routinely evoke God's will, as if to support his decision to go to war with Iraq or his plan to sponsor vastly biased faith-based initiatives. Others condemn gays and lesbi-ans in the name of God, forgetting the very sin they entreat, that of passing judgment. (Mathew 7:1,2 "Do not judge, or you too will be judged. For in the same way you judge others, you will be judged, and with the measure you use, it will be measured to you.") An unlikely sponsor of separating church and state, *The Passion of the Christ* , stands as a ominous reminder of the perils that result when religious leaders take over the roles of judge and jury, and use God to sponsor their political motives.

Another poignant aspect of the film is that Jesus' crucifixion represents the execution of human life, the greatest of sins. The story is a graphic depiction of that which occurs in our very country, all of the time: executing that which we deem frightful. While some might be occasioned to defend the merits of capital punishment, we should remember that under the law of the time, Jesus was a con-victed criminal. In the film, Jesus' nightmarish experience, while appearing forthright and obvious, speaks to us on a very deep, even psychological, level that perpetuates a *naturalized* myth, in Barthes' sense of the word, handed down from generation to generation: society punishes what it does not understand, and kills in the name of fear. Similarly, in Euripides's famed play, *Medea*, when Medea asks Creon why he would banish her before she has committed any crime, he answers simply: "I fear you." And later explains, "I'll act first … in self-defense." This scenario elucidates the manner in which men behave once fear has stricken them and their willingness to forsake their principles in exchange for security; they would rather kill that which they deem expendable, thereby committing the very crime they sought to prevent. Whether it is fear of weapons of mass destruction, gays and lesbians, terrorist plots, criminal behavior, or a disagreement about the existence of God, Jesus shows us, in his refusal to fight even those that strike him down, that humanity is murdered when violence, torture, and execution are employed. But it is the criminal Jesus that gives us hope. Despite the fact he has been beaten by those that rule the law, he proves to be the better man because his humanity, thus his respect for human life, remains. The story of Jesus embodies removing naturalized myths, especially those myths that perpetuate intolerance towards others.

In many ways, Jesus dies not only for the sins of man, but also because of our sinful disposition to kill that which we fear. In this way, Jesus' crucifixion is the cathartic will of a fearful people who employee soldiers to keep their own hands from being soiled. Humankind, in many ways, seems preoccupied with doing harm to his fellow man. But as we see Jesus ascend at the end of the film, we come to realize that enmity imprisons man, and only love, kindness, tolerance, and understanding can procure freedom of conscience.

From a film of this magnitude, a nation such as ours should appreciate the profound truth which the movie presents: cruelty is often sanctioned and lauded when intolerance is allowed to gain footing in a society. Simply put, we can not always blame the government, the President, the military, or even the criminal. Most of us still close our eyes to the swollen face, bleeding body, and closed eye of inhumanity. We sigh with resignation rather than bravely stand for unpopular rightness, swallowing our oath to justice when we know we should cry out. In one form or another, whether with helping hands or closed eyes, we condone Jesus' crucifixion time and time again—only his death pacifies our fears.

Beyond the irrelevant supernaturalism, and the incongruent embellishments made by church fathers, the story of Jesus' life and death speaks to the pious and irreverent alike. And Gibson's film offers us all an opportunity to gain a greater, more profound, even humanistic, understanding of the tragic crucifixion of justice and innocence. The Passion reveals to us our inadequacies in how we treat each other: denying marriage to lovers of the same sex, allowing non-violent offenders to rot in our prisons, preferring to wage war instead of feeding, educating, and providing health care for those in need. It reminds us that we have not yet learned the divine nature of love, brotherhood, and tolerance.

*—A significantly edited version of this work appeared on June 23 2004
in the Humanist Network News.*